Uncover Your Glorious Being

Finding the **Magic in You**

Foreword by Bob Proctor

GLORIA RAMIREZ

Uncover Your Glorious Being

Finding the Magic in You

Foreword by Bob Proctor

GLORIA RAMIREZ

TAG Publishing, LLC
2030 S. Milam
Amarillo, TX 79109
www.TAGPublishers.com
Office (806) 373-0114
Fax (806) 373-4004
info@TAGPublishers.com

ISBN: 978-1-59930-430-4

Text: Lloyd Arbour, www.tablloyd.com

First Edition

Contents

Dedication

I dedicate this book to my sister Maria Angela Ramirez who, through God's grace, became a true mother and Angel in my life.

In Gratitude

I am grateful for the presence of God within me who has, and continues to guide me to the realization of my true essence.

I have received unconditional support from every member of my family including nieces, nephews, my beautiful sisters Maria Angela, Rosalba and Alcira and my wonderful brothers Juan Manuel, Carlos, and Jaime as well as from my mentors, teachers, students, and clients. They have inspired me to uncover my Glorious Being and to find the magic in me. Thank you!

I have profound gratitude for my publishers Elizabeth Ragland and Dee Burks for their patience and especially for their masterful expertise that culminated in the publishing of my book.

The beautiful front and cover of the book was designed by artist Sabrina Fajardo. I have great

respect and gratitude for the quality of her work and for the person she is.

I also wish to thank Dino Pancaro for his priceless assistance in proofreading my book.

Foreword

Gloria Ramirez has experienced more struggle and heartache in her life than some people ever will, yet she's moved forward and is living her life to the fullest in a manner that's worthy of her. Always with a kind word or uplifting story, Gloria has dedicated her life to helping people understand how much power they really have over their lives. She is a serious student of personal and spiritual development and has set many people on the path to a more fulfilling life.

Personal development has been my own life's work and 2014 will mark 53 years from the day I picked up Napoleon Hill's classic, *Think and Grow Rich*. To this day I'm still studying Hill's work and curious to learn more about why we do the things we do and don't do some of the things we know will bring us better results. We all have deep reservoirs of talent and ability lying dormant within - the power of our glorious beings as Gloria calls it - and all we need is the key to unlock this potential. Understanding is the key to freedom and *Uncover Your Glorious Being* will help unlock that key.

Most people want to live their dream and create an abundant life but so many are either afraid or they simply don't know what to do. Gloria is a shining example of what's possible when you make an irrevocable decision to step out of your comfort zone and go for your dreams. It requires guts to do this and a great deal of self discovery … and sometimes that discovery can be painful, on different levels. Gloria encourages each and every person not to hide from challenge or pain and shows the great rewards to be gained by discovering who and what you really are.

Every day, each of us chooses what decisions we will make toward our ultimate success. Or, more to the point, some people don't choose and live by default. When you become consciously aware that you can choose your thoughts and move through your fear rather than just react based on past experience, you put yourself in a position to win and to create the life you want.

Uncover Your Glorious Being shows through example and step-by-step instruction how we can set aside fear and doubt and move beyond obstacles simply by being responsible and taking charge of our lives. There's nothing secret or difficult about change, it just starts with a decision. Gloria's touching and heartfelt stories, along with her words of wisdom, offer a great combination of instruction and encouragement to help you achieve your life-long goals.

Success IS within the reach of every person, no matter their background or circumstance. *Uncover Your Glorious Being* can be a catalyst to help you reach your full potential.

– Bob Proctor,
Teacher in The Secret and
best selling author of *You Were Born Rich*

Introduction

I love to read and have quite a library in my home. Anytime I search for a book, whether in a bookstore or online, I can't help but notice the vast array of subjects regarding personal growth. Books on success, assertiveness, self-esteem, self-control and relationships are everywhere. No matter the issue, there is almost certainly a book specifically written to help. I've spent many years unlearning false truths about myself. Changing my thought processes from unworthy and unlovable to deserving was one of the most challenging and rewarding journeys I have ever taken. I am deserving and worthy of love and so is everyone else.

When I decided to write this book, I asked myself, "What makes *Uncover Your Glorious Being* different from the thousands of personal growth books on the shelves?" Do I have more experience helping people than the other authors? Is my life story compelling enough to inspire a reader? Are these pages just filled with empty words or are they a testament to how I've transformed my life?

With so many personal growth books available, I knew mine had to stand out. After reading several books (too many to count), I noticed one common trait. The majority of the books available only discuss what a content life looks like. They talk about success, love and happiness, but don't give the readers the tools to create the life they've always desired. Before any personal external change can occur, we must first look at ourselves on the inside. Think for a moment about what actually is involved in an internal change. Lasting change is impossible unless we get up close and personal and evaluate our lives, habits, thoughts and actions honestly. An introspective inventory is the foundation to personal and spiritual growth.

Your magic will come alive for you, first with the realization that all change starts with you. Gandhi once said that you have to be the change you want to see in the world. Each one of us has to come to the understanding that only by working on our own issues and healing them we can help others. Each one of us has to take responsibility to clear the blocks to unconditional love. For some of us it is fear, or doubt or judgment. For others it could be lack of forgiveness and even hatred. For others it could be lack of self-esteem, insecurity, lack of self-love. As we heal we embrace our divine essence, the magic in us.

Anyone reading this book is more than likely doing so because they want to be, have and do more. Each page of *Uncover Your Glorious Being* provides not only a glimpse of what fulfillment can look like, but also a complete set of tools needed to grow and live an enriched life. At the end of each chapter, I've included an exercise called Glorious Discovery to teach the reader to learn to forgive, live in the now, love and believe in themselves and manifest their dreams. I know what it is like living with fear, insecurity and anger as well as self-love, peace and joy. I'll take the latter every day. We all deserve a new way of life, and *Uncover Your Glorious Being* is the essential tool to help people find and follow their dreams. A fulfilling life begins with the desire to renew your mind. These pages will give you plenty of inspiration and tools to finding the magic within you.

Chapter 1

Invisible to Invincible

I'm sure you can remember a time in your life that was less than perfect. Throughout everyone's lives, they're faced with difficulties and unexpected events. Life handed me challenges from the moment I was born. Born in Bogota, Colombia, South America, my twin brother, Jaime, and I were the youngest children of seven. My parent's relationship was dysfunctional at best. My Dad lost his father when he was only nine and grew up without a masculine role model and as a result he wasn't able to offer his own children the support and love he missed as a young boy. My mother was raised in an extremely strict household, so she envisioned her marriage to my father as a beautiful life. The fairytale life she dreamed of was shattered by my dad's alcoholism. He continuously came home drunk, leaving her to take care of us all by herself.

Struggling to provide even the simplest of necessities for us each day, I was born into a very unhappy environment. Adding to my mom's surprise, when I came into this world I brought along with me my twin brother Jaime. My brother and I were not planned, five kids were already enough to keep my overly stressed mom busy. She did not have any other choice but to receive us into this world, so she accepted us and did what she could. Filled with the constant worry of her ability to feed two more mouths, Jaime and I were received into this world in very unhappy circumstances. One fact that is certain in life is that there are going to be valleys. I suspect there are indeed many people in this world who get buried in the valleys and don't get as much out of life as they should. What those people don't realize, however, is that for every valley there is a hill. *Climbing the hills of life is what allows you to go from invisible to invincible.*

A World of Uncertainty

Life was challenging at home with my Dad spending money on alcohol that should have been used for food and clothes for such a large family. Disappointed and tired, my mother felt totally alone. My grandparents didn't like my father, so they didn't support her decision to marry him, and she felt completely abandoned by them. Life at home was very difficult for all of us and my mother did not know what to do. She grew up with the belief that marriage was a lifetime contract.

When I was about five, my mother became sick. She made numerous trips to the hospital. My mother was diagnosed with Leukemia. I remember feeling that she was not going to be with me for too long. I felt so sad, I cried constantly. As a little girl I could not imagine my life without my mom. I wanted to spend every waking minute with her. I was terrified that each time she went to the hospital, she would not come home.

I will never forget the day my sisters took my twin brother and I to see her. The hospital bed was so high; I could hardly reach her hands. She stared at Jaime and me with a look of such sadness. I carry that image with me to this day. Mom knew that heaven was calling her home soon. She also realized that she was going to leave behind a ten year old daughter, an eight year old son, and two six year old twins, not to mention my older brother and sisters. The idea of leaving us behind tore her heart into pieces.

My worst fear came true, one day she did not come home. The day before she died, my oldest sister, Maria Angela, visited her. In a couple of months, Maria Angela was to fulfill my mom's goal for her and graduate as an Economist from a very prestigious university. One of Maria Angela's biggest dreams was to share this accomplishment with my mother. During that time, my sister was the only woman to graduate from a class of mostly men, which was very impressive. After graduation, Maria Angela planned to take my mother to Mexico, as this was my mother's big dream.

That night, in a very soft voice, my mother said to her, "I am going to ask you to take care of my kids, my four little ones. I know it is going to be a long road ahead of you and at times you are going to get very tired but you have to continue to be very strong and have faith and you have to promise me that you will not give up. Promise me that you will not abandon them." When life calls you forth for acts of courage, each one of you has the choice to "answer the call" and do what you once thought was impossible. Even though Maria Angela was only in her early twenties, she promised her dying mother to take care of us. The next day my mother passed away.

Maria Angela accomplished her promise victoriously and I am forever grateful. Because my sister answered such a monumental call, her four siblings were loved and cared for until we became respectable adults. I truly believe that my sister Maria Angela was an angel sent from heaven. Now, each one of us has the responsibility to answer our own call and this is exactly what I am doing. When life puts you in situations that are challenging, you have the choice of giving up or stepping up to the plate and answering the call. Remember that you do not have to do it alone. You have an invisible power orchestrating everything for you. The secret is that you have to trust and create a team with your Creator. When faced with uncertainty, know that there is an invisible but very real power ready to support and guide you. All you have to do is ask for guidance, believe and trust.

Not Your Average Cinderella Story

Six months after my mother passed away, my dad remarried. Maria Angela now had a husband and family of her own and since my dad remarried, we were to live with him and his new wife. My stepmother grew increasingly tired of dad's drinking. One night, he came home drunk. As he tried to open the locked door, my stepmother threw a suitcase with his clothes out of the window and told him not to ever come back if he was drunk. That was the last day I saw my dad drunk. She was a very tough person and she was not going to put up with his drinking the way my biological mother did.

I didn't think that life could get worse after my mother died, but I was wrong. Life with my stepmother was the beginning of the most challenging time of my life. The story of Cinderella is nothing compared to what happened to my brother, my sister and me. My stepmother agreed to marry my father on the condition that she didn't have to take care of us. One by one, my father intended to give us away, so he and his new bride could start their life together. The first to go was my twin brother, Jaime. My older brother, Juan Manuel, reluctantly agreed to take Jaime in. He went to live with my seventeen year old brother and his fifteen year old wife. When Maria Angela found out about what our dad was doing, she put a stop to it. She told him that we were his responsibility and he and his new wife had to take care of us. As a result, my brother Carlos, my sister Alcira and I moved in with my father and his wife.

My life with my stepmother was very challenging. She made it obvious that we were not welcome and the only reason we lived with her was because my father forced her to take us in. This was not our home, it was hers and we were treated like second-class beggars. One incident in particular illustrates her anger toward us. My stepmother's grandson was visiting and I was playing with him. She called him into the pantry room and gave him a chocolate bar. I stood there waiting for mine. She looked at me and turned around and walked away. Living with my stepmother was like living in a prison. We had to get up not later than seven in the morning and had to shower immediately. After that we were given a breakfast that lacked any kind of nutrition. I went to school in the afternoon, so the mornings consisted of cleaning the house. Food was not readily available to us. The refrigerator was off limits. We only ate what my stepmother wanted to feed us.

My father allowed her to treat us how ever she wanted. My brother and sister and I were well-behaved children who just wanted a happy life. We did what we were told for the most part, although she didn't see it that way. Many times, my father spanked me with a belt because my stepmother made something up about my behavior. What made it more tolerable was that my brother Carlos, who was two years older and my sister Alcira, who was four years older, lived with mc. We gave each other the support we needed to make our lives bearable.

Life was difficult for the three of us living with my dad and stepmother, but it was worse for my twin brother Jaime who had to face his own challenges. His caretaker, my brother Juan Manuel, had his own hills to climb with three children and a very young wife. Jaime felt so rejected and unloved because of the death of his mother and the separation from his siblings and his twin sister that he ran away from home several times to live in the streets of Bogota. Experiences that are so traumatic in a child's life can create deep wounds. However, once you become an adult, you have the responsibility to love yourself enough to want to heal the past and create a new beautiful life for yourself. When you are faced with difficult situations in life you can become bitter or better. It is your choice. When life hands you adversity, face it head on and take advantage of your struggles to become a stronger, more steadfast person.

There Are Angels Among Us

After seven years, my stepmother had enough of us. One day I finally had the courage to complain about an incident and this prompted a huge argument between my father and my stepmother over us living with them. He relented and she threw us out. My father agreed to find an apartment and pay the rent for my younger brother, my sister and me. I was fifteen when all of this happened. We spent the first night huddled together crying tears of joy because we were happy that we had been liberated. My brother and sister thanked me for liberating them from the emotional and physical abuse we had all been through. In reality I was the reason my stepmother threw us out. We were free. Free to eat what we wanted, free to talk on the phone and free to live.

My father only paid one month's rent. We didn't know what to do until our guardian angel saved us. My oldest sister, Maria Angela stepped up to become our new mom. She taught me that God always sends us angels to care for us. She became our mom in every meaning of this word. Life at home with my dad and stepmother was hard and she felt great pain for the suffering we had to endure. She felt so guilty for not being able to help and would cry every day just by thinking about the way we were treated at home.

She made sure we had enough to eat and anything else we needed. She attended all events at school, including Mother's Day celebrations. She was very strict about education because she knew that was our ticket to a better life. I remember looking forward to the end of every school year because Maria Angela always gave me a present. One time she showed up with a beautiful watch and I was in heaven. I was a great student so she always acknowledged me for my accomplishments. She also made sure that we had some type of entertainment on the weekends and most of the time she would take us to a park, or to have ice cream and sometimes she would send us to the movies.

I remember so well how much I liked when she took us to a place called Café Yanuba. For years she took us to this wonderful place. When I was little I used to ask for ice cream, most of the time one called Peach Melba with banana. I loved it. As I grew up I used to order tea, the way English people serve it with milk. The wait staff would come with a tray of pastries and I would order my favorite one. This café was very sophisticated and offered great service. Maria Angela enjoys the finer aspects of life and she always gave us the chance to have the best whenever it was feasible for her. She was and still is my role model and I will cherish her forever.

The other angel that I had in my life was my sister Rosalba. Just a couple of years younger than Maria Angela, she made it a point to support us. She and Maria Angela teamed up to help take care of our daily needs. Rosalba was a person with a very beautiful heart. Even though she had her own family, husband, kids and still took the time to take care of us. She took us to the doctor and on trips with her family. I loved going to visit her because she treated me with so much love. In fact everyone used to tell her not to spoil me so much. She just wanted to protect me like she was my mother. She also had a difficult time knowing that we were not being taken care off well by my dad and stepmother. The moments we spent with my sisters were very precious to us. I also have deep gratitude for my brother Carlos and my sister Alcira who lived with me. In my eyes they are heroes. They were both working and going to school full time, so they could provide for the three of us.

God sent them to me and I will be forever grateful for them. Life calls you forth to courageous acts. You have to remember that you have the power within to answer the call. Take the time to think of the angels in your life. Feel gratitude in your heart for the way they impacted your life and for teaching you to be an angel in someone else's life.

Ascending the Hill to Greatness

The messages given to me by my dad and stepmother conditioned me to think negatively throughout my life. As a young girl, I lived with the constant reminder that I was unwanted, unworthy of love and invisible. They tried to get me in a physical prison, but no one, no matter how hard they try, can keep you in a mental prison. With my sisters' encouragement, I moved from invisible to invincible. Challenges and obstacles try to take away our life but they don't have to. When we don't understand why life is working out for us, we need to focus on climbing the hill, just like my mother did before she died.

One of my mom's strongest characteristics was her ambition. Despite an unhappy marriage and lack of support, she loved us and worked very hard to give all of her children the best life possible. One of her primary goals for us was to get an education because in her family the daughters weren't allowed to go to college after high school. Her drive for us to go to college was so strong that she did not allow any of my older sisters to help her in the kitchen because she wanted them to study. I am proud to say because of my mother's intention, all of my brothers and sisters have undergraduate and master's degrees.

I remember one time I didn't want to go to school so I hid my uniform underneath my mattress. Mom found the outfit, immediately dressed me and took me to school. I didn't want to go to school; I wanted to stay with my mother. No matter the excuse, my brothers, sisters and I had to go to school because she believed that if we had an education we could support ourselves and not have to go through the struggles she went through. I am grateful for her insistence of us going to school because she taught us discipline and persistence, which have been vital in my journey on earth.

One of the things I love to do is to recall the ways God has brought me to the place where I am today. Have you ever done that? Have you ever reflected on the events and people God used in your past to help you become the person you are today? I encourage you to take time today or this week to remember the people and circumstances God placed in your life. I am grateful for every single instance, both good and challenging or difficult, in my life. I treasure my name Gloria, because it feels like with my name I am glorifying my Creator. He draws us to Himself and gives us unconditional love so that we can share His love with others.

When life becomes a constant battle we must continue on our journey up the hill. With endless persistence and determination we can move onward and upward. We must persist with faith, forgiveness and love. We must keep the right attitude toward life and toward God, live with courage and tap into our internal strength. I will be sharing with you in subsequent chapters how I freed myself by going through what I call an "awakening process" where I had the chance to forgive everyone and everything for what happened in my childhood. I took my experiences and used them to help others who have been hurt while my brother, Jaime, traveled down a darker path of "victimhood".

You have to learn to have compassion and live life as a victor, not a victim. No matter your circumstance or situation, it is time to take a hold of a life full of love and apply that mindset to all your relationships. If it's something good, keep it in your heart and mind. If it's something bad that someone has done to you, let it wash over you. Some people spend their entire lives focusing on their past. They wonder why they didn't do well in school, why their parents didn't treat them in a certain way or anything else that didn't go as planned.

There is an important principle in life known as sowing and reaping. A farmer is a good example of this principle. Through hard work and care of his fields, he'll receive a bountiful crop. However, if he doesn't tend to his crops, his harvest will suffer. The same is true with life. If you sow good thoughts and positivity, you'll reap the same. But if you go around sowing negativity, anger and hatred in life then that's what you'll receive in return. You can't sow bad and expect good. It doesn't work that way, so you must make it your aim in life to do good, to treat people with love and then you'll reap abundance. Tough times will come, but with the right perspective and attitude, you can ascend the hill to greatness.

Regardless of the circumstances that you are born into, you have the ability to create a miraculous life. The pages that follow will reveal to you how to let go and let your greatness show. Although I felt invisible to my mom and my dad because of what was going on at home, in the following chapters I will share with you how your first priority is to be visible to yourself so you can become invincible to the world.

— *Glorious Discovery* —

- Take the time to think of the angels in your life. Feel gratitude in your heart for the way they impacted your life and for teaching you to be an angel in someone else's life.

- Reflect on the events and people God has placed in your life to help you become the person you are today.

- Regardless of the circumstances that you are born into, you have the ability to create a miraculous life. Team up with your Creator and trust and believe in your ability to create a beautiful life.

Affirm:

- I embrace life with love and joy. I am invincible

- I am grateful for every single experience in my life

- I am grateful for all the angels in my life

- I have the power to create a Glorious life

- I am a victor

Chapter 2

The Search for Fulfillment

Just before I graduated from college (Economics & Business Administration), my sister Maria Angela shared with me that she had always wanted to come to the United States to learn English but she never had the chance because of her responsibilities with her children and us, her siblings. She said, "If you accept, I am happy to provide for all of your expenses and education there including learning the language and pursuing an MBA." I of course said yes, and a few weeks later I sailed to the USA. I learned to speak English and forged a new life for myself. The world was wide open for me. Finally, I had the fresh start to create a wonderful life for myself. The problem was that my life in America didn't turn out exactly as I planned. Divorced twice, I was unhappy, angry and unable to forgive. The reason I was in this space was because although I was not living in my home country, I was carrying with me my childhood experiences and I did not know it.

Do you spend your days in a state of unhappiness, worry and complacency? How many times have you run from stressful or painful situations in your life and try to escape pain and hurt by moving to another city, changing jobs or through relationships? Many times people confuse drastic changes with permanent solutions only to find out years later that all of the pain and despair is still alive on the inside. I encourage you to ask yourself, "do I invest my days in a state of trust, serenity and happiness?"

You aren't meant to just exist; instead, you are meant to create and thrive. It is part of your natural instinct to want more out of life, but unfortunately you may have been conditioned to find excuses or reasons why a new way of living is impossible. Whose fault is it? Not mine? I didn't do it? If only my childhood had been different. Do any of these sound familiar? For many years, I blamed my stepmother and father for my problems. It was easier for me to use them as scapegoats than to take an honest look at myself. I didn't want to accept responsibility and admit that my life lacked fulfillment because of my inability to get in touch with my emotions. My life moved forward because I owned up to my thoughts, behaviors and actions.

You must learn to take responsibility and instead of feeling like you are a victim, affirm that you are "a victor". Once you let go of past hurts, stop making excuses and quit comparing yourself with others, fulfillment is inevitable. Each day affirm to yourself that it is your birthright to live a fulfilled life.

Let Go with Love

Some people carry past hurts or grudges with them throughout their lives. My second marriage was less than a storybook romance. The more I pretended my marriage was happy, the worse I felt. After a few months the arguments between my husband and myself escalated to the point of verbal violence and one time he pushed me and I pushed him back. This incident made me realize that I had to seek help. My sister-in-law, Judit (who will always have my deepest gratitude), knew my relationship was in trouble and recommended I visit a support group called Al-Anon. I did not go because I was in complete denial about the gravity of the situation. Then the inevitable happened: our marriage ended in divorce. I finally started going to the meetings because I realized I needed help. During the first month I attended daily meetings and cried at every one. The more meetings I attended, the more I realized, as I listened to other people tell their stories, that I was not the only one facing these types of challenges. There were other people going through a similar experience. Al-Anon helped me to discover that I had been carrying a great deal of anger and hurt from my childhood. I carried the weight of my abuse with me into every relationship. I needed to release my pain and forgive my father and stepmother. Once I came to this realization, I decided to start Al-Anon's life-altering twelve-step program and find a sponsor who would work with me to learn and truly apply the steps in my life. I vividly remember asking my sponsor, Billie Beth, a beautiful lady, who was a veteran at the meetings, to help me with the process of the twelve steps. She agreed, but could only work with me five minutes a week. The first assignment that she gave me was to write down all of the things that were unmanageable in my life.

Some steps took several weeks and others took less time. Each of the twelve steps' assignments Billie Beth gave me was healing my life in ways that were truly miraculous. I was very diligent with each of my assignments and Billie Beth was quite impressed with my level of commitment. It was a deep and intense process but the improvement that I was experiencing kept me going and wanting more. During the time I went through these twelve steps, I realized that when a person is too close to an event they can't see the entire situation. I like to tell my clients that if they stand in a picture they can't see the frame, which is why you have to ask for help to see another perspective of the solution so you can heal it.

After I finished all twelve steps, my life was completely transformed. My life-altering experience gave me the inspiration to create "The Twelve Step Mastery Coaching Program", which is my signature program. Throughout the course of my coaching career, I have been privileged to witness many powerful transformations in my clients and their families as a result of these twelve steps.

Any painful experiences that occurred during your childhood or as an adult can be released. You have to have the humility to accept help. After I forgave my stepmother and father for all they had done, I was able to let go of my anger and made a commitment to maintain a positive outlook on life. An optimistic attitude is crucial during the process of releasing past anguish. The majority of your actions have been based on the past and until you can let go of what happened, your dreams will be just that -dreams. My inability to forgive caused me to be temperamental, have financial problems and be unable to show affection toward anyone. I really didn't realize how much it negatively influenced every aspect of my life. When I finally released my past, my dreams turned into reality.

You have the choice to let go of the pain from those events and progress forward. At the end of the day it is your choice to be a victim or a victor. Regardless of whether your life story is similar to mine or entirely different, all that matters is that you can let go of your past and create a beautiful life. If you don't like how your life has turned out, then determine what areas need to change. From this moment on, think about what you truly desire most in this wonderful life. Perhaps you are in the middle of resurrecting your life right now. Some of you are trying to rebuild the trust in your marriage. Or you may be trying to rebuild your career, or your finances, or perhaps your sense of confidence. And you're starting to wonder if you're dealing with an impossible situation. If you truly believe in yourself and your abilities, nothing is impossible. Unfortunately, many times the details of day to day living can create a barrier between you and your happiness. No deadlines, commitments, distractions or obstacles have the power to prevent you from finding the fulfillment you deserve. You owe it to yourself to find peace and the moment is now, not tomorrow or any other time. Let go with love and embrace your happiness.

Honor Your Emotions

Ours is a society built on comfort. Walk into any furniture store, and notice the chairs with heaters and massagers along with built-in drink holders, magazine pouches and remote control holders. Movie theaters have luxurious seating. Even airlines are advertising comfortable seating. You are conditioned to be comfortable. The question you need to ask yourself is, "What is the source of your comfort?" Do you have permanent comfort or temporary comfort? What does it mean to be temporary? It won't last long. Temporary comfort is fleeting. Comfortable living is wonderful, as long as you don't become slaves of it. Permanent comfort is more intangible. For example, the satisfaction of expressing love and compassion leads to joy in your heart for helping others.

Temporary comfort goes away. It doesn't last forever. The world needs happier and more satisfied people and each one of you has the responsibility of being the change you want to see in the world. People everywhere are looking for answers to the emptiness they feel inside. They will do anything to fill their void even if it only brings them a short time of satisfaction or happiness. So, what is the solution? Materialism and wealth? Pleasure and enjoyment? Power and prestige? There is an answer to the eternal question, "How do I find happiness and fulfillment in my life?" A life that is complete comes only when you learn to honor your emotions.

People who enjoy the abundant life possess all of these qualities: love, joy, peace, patience, kindness, goodness, faithfulness, gentleness, self-control, compassion, purity, humility, forgiveness, faith, character, wisdom, enthusiasm, dignity, optimism, confidence and honesty. People who consciously demonstrate these qualities in their daily living enjoy a beautiful relationship with their Creator. A fulfilled life is full of all the items money can't buy. No matter how much money you have, you cannot buy more patience, self-control, or peace! You already possess the qualities within yourself. All you have to do is awaken them in you. You can reawaken the above attributes by getting in touch with your emotions.

I used to carry a good deal of baggage. Chances are so do you. Emotional baggage is a part of life. Once you honor your emotions, you no longer carry any unnecessary past thoughts. You cannot fall into the trap of complacency. You must constantly strive to grow. Change is never comfortable. Are you willing to honor your emotions and take complete control over them? Are you willing to make this your first priority in your life, ahead of everything else? If you answered yes, then journaling is one of the best methods to honor your emotions. When you journal, you hand over your unwanted feelings over to your Creator.

Journaling helped me overcome my reoccurring feelings about my childhood and was instrumental in helping me heal the pain of going through my divorces. Journaling is also a great tool to write about your positive experiences and feelings. I wrote my feelings every day because it was a time of healing. It is just a process of helping you move into a period of tranquility. Working on the past is a gift you give yourself and it will morph you into the present time. When a situation or event happens that brings back any old thoughts, don't fall back into your old way of acting. Instead, take a moment and journal your feelings. Whenever I wake up feeling bad, I write those feelings down. By doing so, I've given them up and don't carry them with me for the rest of the day. Make the decision to be happy and don't let negative emotions drag you down during the day. You have the power within you to do this when you journal. Little by little, journaling will help your pain, sadness and anger to slip away so you can be, have and do anything you want.

Some other ways to honor your emotions are through meditation, going for a walk with nature, listening to classical music, hiring a coach. Also, to release any anger you can be in a room by yourself and yell or scream or hit a pillow to let out the pain. These are healthy methods to release your emotions. Whenever you deal with strong emotions affirm to yourself that you honor your emotions because they are a doorway to your happiness.

You Have Value

Each one of you has specific talents and special gifts to offer the world. The problem is that some people don't believe in their abilities because they constantly compare themselves with other people. You think you aren't as good as your sister because they have a bigger house or your neighbor has more money because they drive a better car. When you compare yourself with your siblings or others it is difficult. The trouble with comparisons is that they create a face of insecurity and thought of *am I good enough*? After my mother died, my sister told my teacher that I didn't have a mother and to please be kind to me. The teacher turned around and told the other kids that I didn't have a mother and it caused me a lot of embarrassment and envy for the kids that did have mothers. It bothered me so badly that I asked my sister to move me to another school. When I finally did move to another school, I never told anyone and I trusted my sister would not tell anyone either. I came up with lies all the time when kids asked me about my mother. I grew up thinking that it was better to hide the truth so I did not feel embarrassed.

I really did a good job of scrutinizing my life for a long time. I didn't feel as good as the other children because I didn't have a mother. It was like I was a nobody and I started feeling inferior because of this. Some of the kids may have felt as though they were inadequate because the mother and father were divorced and they weren't a family and then felt inferior. Unfortunately, society promotes comparisons. Do you always want to be as thin as the latest supermodel or as rich as the best actor? Comparing yourself can make you feel inferior for a myriad of reasons, but the good news is you don't have to feel this way because you are perfect in the Creator's image.

The only way to defeat comparisons is to believe in yourself and have complete security in who you are. Through coaching, reading books, and attending seminars, I started to learn that I was my own person. I began to accept my inner beauty and to understand and embrace my true essence, which is love. That's when the comparisons started to fade away. After I attended Al-Anon for a couple of years, I came to the realization that I was worthy of all that God had to offer and that my past did not have to be a reflection of my future. Let me ask you this, if you don't believe in yourself, then how can you consider your life as a gift? You count, you are important, you make a difference. You are a gift to the world. Your journey is to believe in yourself so you accept these truths.

Once you start working on yourself and gain more self-confidence, you are not affected by the opinions of others. When you have self-confidence, you embrace your essence. Individuality is a gift from God. If He planned to make all of us the same, how boring that would be? Some have the gift of painting and I have the gift of healing. The Creator made us unique with our own talents and gifts. It is up to you to discover your talents and share them with others. You have to realize what you do well and give yourself permission to express it through your profession, hobby or activities. The reason why you are here on earth is to express your uniqueness. Being unique is a great gift. The more you embrace your gifts the more they will give you creativity and the confidence to share them with others.

I've heard it said before that our Creator will take away our gifts if you don't use them. I don't believe this for a minute. God is pure love so He would never take anything away from you, He is pure love. God is patience. He doesn't care if he has to wait an entire lifetime for you to discover your gifts. I remember attending a seminar one time when my mentor, motivational speaker Les Brown, asked the audience where the richest place in the world was. No one had the answer. He told us it was the cemetery. The room was very quiet for a time and then he asked, "Why was it the richest place in the world." Then he said, "It has books in it that were never written, poems that were not recited and beautiful opportunities that were not fulfilled. There were dancers that had an innate gift that never gave themselves permission to be brave and share their gift. There were songs that were never sung." Then he asked, "What do you want to do with your life?" The room was in total silence again, and I thought *oh my, his words are so powerful.*

You have the responsibility to honor God, the giver and your gift. I remember a young lady in the audience told Les that she felt a void in her life because she stopped singing. She sang almost every day, especially in her church. He said, "Come over here to the stage young lady." She sang "Amazing Grace" and you wouldn't imagine how quiet the audience was. You could hardly hear the people around you breathing. He told her when she was finished that it was an abomination to God not to share this gift. Les then asked her to promise that she was going to share her gift with humanity. After he finished talking to her, he turned to the audience and told all of us, "You cannot rob humanity of your gifts and talents. It is your responsibility to share them with the world." Life is always asking you to participate and you pretend that you don't hear it and look the other way. I waited too long to work on this book because I could hear my stepmother telling me I wasn't good enough. I am good enough to do anything I want and so are you.

If I hadn't discovered God's gifts, I would be living a life of desperation, sorrow, mediocrity and fear. Those words conjure sorrow and frustration to me because I know now how good my life is and can't stand the thought of anyone else living an unfulfilled life. The pain of separation from my second husband was so great that it really pushed me to find my gift. I am meant to help people and remind them of the glorious being that resides inside of them. I love to work with young people and have recently started work on opening an orphanage in Ghana, Africa. I am now filled with love and gratitude. I rebuilt my life and now live each day to the fullest. My wish is for everyone to get out of bed with the same enthusiasm as I do and go through each day with the knowledge that God made them to be unique and to offer value. Affirm to yourself that you are a gift to the world and you count and make a difference.

— Glorious Discovery —

- Let go of the past with Love

  - If the results in your life are not satisfactory, help yourself by willing to seek help. Take action and trust in the process.

- Daily honor your emotions with love and compassion

  - Journaling can help you release unhealed emotions. Write about your feelings and any painful memories from the past with the intention of letting go to embrace the new you.

  - Focus on spreading love.

  - Make the decision to be happy.

- Know that You Have Value

  - To discover your gifts and talents write about what you love doing and affirm that every day you have more clarity about your mission and reason for being here on earth.

  - Be proud of your God given gifts and talents and share them with humanity.

  - You are unique. You count. You make a difference.

Affirm:

- I take responsibility for my life
- I honor my emotions. They are my doorway to my happiness
- I am proud to share my gifts and talents
- I believe in myself
- I am a gift to the world

Chapter 3

Mindful Living

I am grateful for all the tools and self-development practices that have taught me to clean the garden of my heart. The twelve-step program helped me to release anger and replace it with forgiveness; to release fear and replace it with faith; to release criticism and replace it with love. Several years passed until I was able to get to the point that I could feel love in my heart again. Once I realized that I blamed others for all of my problems and expected them to create my life for me, I knew it was time to make some dramatic changes. I could no longer live in robotic mode and spend each day on autopilot following the crowd. In my search for answers, I came across a Winston Churchill quote that intrigued me. He stated that *the power of the mind is what makes things happen.* His words encouraged me to explore the mind further. Through the course of my studies, I met

Bob Proctor, who became my mentor, and I joined his LifeSuccess Consulting group and got certified to teach his programs. His lessons taught me that the mind is the most powerful tool in creation.

When I took responsibility, I noticed my life improving. "Knowing" is key in changing your life. Because the truth is, obstacles and challenges are a part of life. But if you are willing to believe that you can create with your mind, then you will find evidence every day in both large and small ways. Once you experience the true power of taking responsibility you will understand how sweet that experience is.

It is extremely important to know the mind, because it is said that you become what you think about. I take this quite seriously because philosophers, theologians, and great thinkers all agree that you become what you think about. So, it is vital to understand the mind, embrace its powers and work with it, so we can manifest in our lives what we want to accomplish. You must study the mind every day so that you understand who you are and the ability you have to tap into the infinite power available to you. Once you grasp this concept, life is a wonderful journey of new and exciting experiences. Embrace the power of your mind to create a joyful living.

A New Sense of Empowerment

From the moment of my revelation of the powers of the magnificent mind, I was empowered to learn all that I could about it. So I studied every day to learn anything and everything about the mind. Bob Proctor's explanation of the mind is one of the best I've ever heard. His presentations using the Stickman illustration of the mind (originally created by Dr. Thurman Fleet) really taught me about the power of the mind and gave me the understanding of the infinite potential that resides inside of me. Now I'd like to share the image of the Stickman with you.

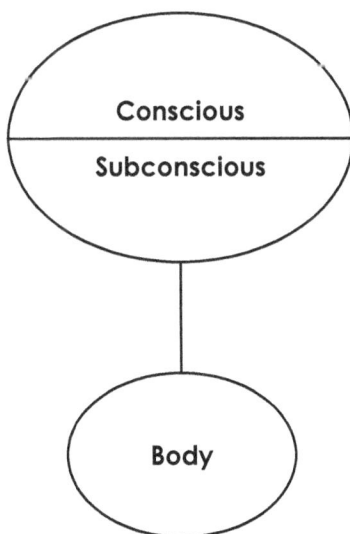

Conscious

Subconscious

Body

As you may have noticed, the mind is divided into two distinct parts. The top half is the conscious mind and the bottom section is the subconscious mind. The conscious mind is the thinking mind that gives you the free will to do certain actions or behaviors. It receives your thoughts and determines whether to accept or reject them. For instance, I decided not to watch television any more because of all the negativity in the media. This idea was due to my conscious mind allowing me to accept only ideas that empowered my life. This one small decision helped me to realize that I had the power to accept only positive facts and information into my mind. I haven't watched the news for many years. It is imperative for you to make a constant effort to pay attention to the ideas you have to either accept or reject them. Another way to take responsibility for what you put in your mind is to participate in positive conversations and to associate with like-minded people.

The conscious mind initiates your thoughts while the subconscious, on the other hand, carries them out. I like to refer to the conscious mind as the gardener and the subconscious mind as the garden. The gardener is the conscious mind and they can decide what to plant in their garden (the subconscious mind). I've used this theory to clean out my garden and remove the weeds in my heart so that I could rid my subconscious mind of the many generations of limiting thoughts that were implanted there.

I also learned that the subconscious mind doesn't know the difference between what's real and what's not. Pause for a moment to absorb this concept and its implications. If the subconscious mind can't tell the difference between fact or fiction, then it is crucial to be aware of what we are feeding into it. If we are feeding lies, negativity and harmful thoughts to our conscious mind, our subconscious accepts them and we experience these unpleasant things in our lives. However, if we feed truth, positive and loving thoughts to our conscious mind, our subconscious will accept them and we will create beauty in our lives. What we see created in our lives is a direct result of what we put into our minds.

Another interesting aspect of the subconscious mind is that it never stops working. All of my feelings of inferiority and unworthiness bombarded my subconscious mind twenty-four hours a day three hundred sixty five days a year! No wonder I was temperamental and depressed. This newfound knowledge enabled me to look at my current beliefs and decide if they were accurate or not. The weeds or insecurities growing in my mind kept me from accomplishing my goals. Now, I only accept ideas or thoughts that are useful to me. You can use the power of affirmations or repetition to replace any negative thoughts with productive and encouraging ones. They will be received by your subconscious mind and this will become your new reality. I like to tell my clients to fill their mind with a fresh clean stream of continuous beautiful thoughts to flush out the contaminated ones. Fill your mind with empowering thoughts every second of the day.

It's a Beautiful Day

Now that I have a clear understanding of how the mind works, I rely much more on my imagination to plant seeds in my garden. Author, Napoleon Hill, says that the imagination puts useful ideas into the subconscious and since it can't distinguish between real and unreal it can be a powerful tool to help you achieve your goals. Working with the conscious and subconscious mind helps you to live a more productive life. This is what I do every day to help me get to where I want to be.

My life is so much more fulfilled now because I no longer live in ignorance. Some people don't like hearing that word because they believe it means stupid. Quite the contrary, when a person is ignorant they don't know *how* to change. I lived in ignorance for a good portion of my life. When we don't understand the conscious and subconscious mind and how they work, we are living in ignorance because we are accepting what other people say and believe about us as truth. For example, when the economy of a country is not at its best, people believe that there in a "bad economy" because there are not eneough jobs, the real estate market is down and there is no money. The truth is that you have the internal power to create your own economy. You have to realize that your thoughts are creating your reality. If you accept what the media, co-workers, friends and family tell you as truth then you are truly living in ignorance.

When you operate from the state of ignorance you are also in the state of fear.

Choose to operate from the state of understanding and do not live in the state of fear. When adversity shows up in your life, you just need to take a look at your thoughts because they are creating your sense of reality. Your thoughts will produce what you want. If you want perfect health, more happiness and wealth, choose thoughts that are in alignment with your desires. That is what I do regardless of appearances and this is why my life has been good, because every day I'm moving into more understanding of my mind and I realize that I have the power within to change anything.

You receive ideas into the conscious mind every second of the day from both internal and external sources. The good news is now that you understand the mind, you have the power to choose which thoughts enter your subconscious mind. For example when you wake up in the morning and decide that your day is going to be unpleasant, you've just programmed your subconscious to make that idea come true. But if you wake up thinking this is going to be the best day ever, you've just fed your subconscious mind an idea that will reward you with a wonderful treat that can be experienced through your body and that's the energy you will send out. This is the Law of Vibration operating in your life. As you send out this vibration, the law of attraction responds with like kind experiences. It is important to remember that your subconscious mind doesn't have the power to accept or reject thoughts, so if your conscious mind tells you that something is going to be a beautiful experience, it will be.

To become a leader in your field you have to take responsibility for the events in your life. I lived in ignorance for many years and when I began to understand the mind I was able to move to another level. That's when I really started to recognize that I could use my mind to accomplish what I wanted. You can use your mind to believe that your dream has already come true. When you awaken to the truth, then the truth will set you free and this is how you regain your power to achieve anything you want. Just like I did and still do, so can you use the power of your mind to create whatever you want. You too are in control of your destiny. When you have that faith then your life keeps expanding. By understanding the mind, you are able to live a life of understanding and work around any type of circumstance. What a beautiful thought to know that all you've ever dreamed of is within your grasp. Each day tell yourself that today is the best day of your life.

Thinking on a Higher Level

Rene Descartes once said that, "It is not enough to have a good mind; the main thing is to use it well." This is an important quote because you have been conditioned from an early age to allow what you see, hear, smell, taste and touch to direct your thoughts and actions instead of consciously making choices about what you are constantly being bombarded with. We allow TV, radio, the newspapers and other people to dictate how we think and feel. The author of *The 7 Habits of Highly Effective People*, Stephen R. Covey stated it this way: "Our ultimate freedom is the right and power to decide how anybody or anything outside ourselves will affect us." This is where your conscious or intellectual mind needs to be exercised, to help you to be in control of your mind, not letting the outside world control your emotions and actions.

These Intellectual Factors in our inner world are Perception, Will, Imagination, Memory, Intuition and Reason. If you want different results, to have more – be more – do more - you need to learn more about these and then you can use them to decide and determine what thoughts to allow into your mind. Just as I did with the conscious and subconscious minds, I'm going to discuss these individually as well.

Perception. Perception refers to the way we perceive the world around us. We gather information through our five senses, and perception adds meaning to that information. Take for example the change in perception you would have viewing your world by wearing sunglasses with pink lenses compared to sunglasses with dark lenses. The way you see the world would be quite different.

Most people assume that they see with their eyes. This is not an accurate understanding. You actually see through your eyes. All your eyes are doing is relaying information to your brain and then it interprets what you see. This interpretation is often distorted by our memories and beliefs. A situation, circumstance or event can have a totally different meaning by two different people. For example, a couple can go into a coffee shop to get a mocha latte and one person thinks the clerk was rude because they didn't chat while the other person thinks that they were just being efficient. Perception largely determines your thoughts and actions. More often than not your perception is based on your past experiences.

I read somewhere about the biology of 'seeing' and how a person never sees anything directly, but instead the light waves enter the eyes and are reflected first through a part of the mind that holds all experiences and associations with a specific memory. Each one of you hardly ever sees anything that has not been colored by your previous experiences. No matter your age or background, you make associations in regards to your perception.

For most of my life I had the wrong perception about losing my mother at the age of six and a half. I felt victim of a very sad experience and I perceived it as something very bad that happened to me. Years later when I started to let go of ignorance and had more understanding that adversity doesn't happen to you but instead it happens for you, I was willing to have a new perception of my mom's death. One day, in front of an audience in a seminar, I thanked my mom for leaving me at such early age. I shared that her absence in my life forced me to learn many qualities, including independence, self-reliance, trust and compassion for others going through similar experiences. I also expressed how I learned to love others with the love that I did not have, the love of a mother. At that moment I shifted my perception from one of victim to one of acceptance. I came into the understanding that this was part of a divine order unfolding for my highest good.

The majority of your reality only exists because you were taught it existed. You are conditioned to think a certain way. A person from a different culture may think looking you in the eye is a sign of disrespect while another culture believes just the opposite. Perception is individual. It doesn't mean that one person is right and the rest are wrong, it just displays that your interpretations are often as unique and individual as snowflakes. Experience follows perception. Your experiences depend on your perception, and what you perceive may or may not have anything to do with what really is. Instead it has more to do with what you have been taught. How much does your conditioning affect the experiences in your life? If you want a better experience in life, what can you do? Simply change your perception and change your life!

Will. Every day, our will is tested. It doesn't matter if it is with a scrumptious piece of chocolate

cake or if it is to hit the snooze bar one more time in the morning. We have to decide between what we know we should do and what we want to do. The ability to resist temptations is commonly described as self-control or willpower. Will is essentially a mental muscle, and certain physical and mental forces can weaken or strengthen our self-control. Learning to strengthen our will produces a positive effect in our life.

There have been many times when I have exercised my mental muscle. One time in particular remains with me to this day, and it was right after I finished my studies at the university in Colombia. As I mentioned in the previous chapter, my sister Maria Angela gave me the gift to come to United States. I felt a huge sense of responsibility once I arrived in this country and had to use the power of will all those times when I missed my family so much that I wanted to leave everything behind and jump on a plane and go back to my family. There were many tears shed debating between taking advantage of this wonderful opportunity my sister was giving me or abandoning everything at once. It was so difficult and I am so happy that by exercising my intellectual faculty of will, I was able to not only learn the language fluently but also finish my master's degree in business administration. I continue exercising the power of will every time I miss my family, knowing that for now I have a mission to complete and I willingly embrace this journey.

Imagination. Everything is created twice – once through the imagination of a thought and then in reality. Imagination is the ability to look at any situation from a different point of view (perception), and enables you to create your own reality. When you use your imagination, you're using more than just your ability to see an image. Imagination includes all of your five senses as well as your feelings. When you imagine your perfect life you need to not only think about what it looks like but what it smells, feels, tastes and sounds like, too.

I use the faculty of my imagination on a daily basis because as Albert Einstein once said, "Imagination is everything. It is the preview of life's coming attractions." One of the projects that I am part of is to build self-sustainable homes for children who have lost their parents. How I got to be part of this project was the result of pure imagination. First I had the desire to help orphaned children because I was an orphan myself. Then, in 2004, I was guided to start Glorious Being Center, a not-for-profit organization, which has the purpose to empower children and women to greatness. As I gave myself permission to dream big, the universe has conspired in my favor to bring me the resources, people, funds and opportunities to make my dream a reality. I imagined myself visiting the children in their new home, eating their food, hearing them singing, hugging them and involving all my senses in the process, and recently I went to Ghana, Africa to help the women and children I saw in my imagination. It is important to remember that God is in charge of the "how" and all you have to do is trust and imagine that you already have what you desire. Each one of us possesses the faculty of imagination. You just have to practice using it to perfect it. Imagination enables you to reach all of your goals and overcome any obstacles. Using your imaginative skills doesn't mean you waste your time daydreaming; instead, it gives you a strong creative force to recreate your destiny. When you understand how to harness the power of your imagination, you are on the path to success and fulfillment. What does your imagination say about your ideal life? Create your vision as if you are already living it.

Memory. Memory is your ability to store and recall past experiences. My mentor, Bob Proctor, always says, "Most people are operating under the impression they have a poor memory. We all have perfect memory, it is just weak." So how do you make something weak become strong? First, you must exercise it just as with any other muscle in your body.

As you learned earlier, the subconscious mind is the warehouse where all memories and experiences are stored. All information that comes to you is stored in your subconscious mind. Your conscious mind is what you use to retrieve the information that has been stored. Indeed all the memories are stored in that warehouse, but whether you are able to retrieve that information or not remains a different story. What makes information retrievable? How can you remember different bits of information? Well, this is where developing your mental faculty of memory comes into play.

In the same way you can reframe your perception through an association, you can also improve your memory. Information is remembered by creating an association. This association is like a road map guiding you to where all of your information is stored. Imagine for a moment that you lost your cell phone. You rummage around the entire house thinking *where did I put this thing* while deep in your subconscious mind, you know where you left it. But because no association was made, you don't remember where you put it.

As a speaker, I make great effort to memorize names because for me it shows a sign of respect. I genuinely care about each person that I meet. I purposely repeat their name to make sure I pronounce it correctly and to store it in

Uncover Your Glorious Being

my subconscious mind. Through repetition, my ability to memorize people's names is becoming easier each time I meet someone. By remembering names, I am developing more quality relationships with people. They notice when you care enough to at least remember their names. I also ask questions and pay attention attentively so I can use what they share with me to show that I care.

Another memorization practice I enjoy is to memorize quotes. I have great love for them and I enjoy sharing them with audiences or clients because I notice how they help to create a shift in their thinking. I notice that the more I choose to memorize quotes the easier it becomes. The ability to exercise the memory muscle is crucial because this is the way you register it in your subconscious mind right away and it will be available to access later on when you need to. If your mind wants to say to you, "I don't remember", you can answer back, "I choose to remember" and then you will.

Intuition. Call it a hunch, gut feeling or that little nagging voice; I'm certain you have experienced intuition at one time or another. Intuition is one of the greatest mental faculties because it is another way of seeing the truth. Intuition communicates with you through symbols, feelings and emotions. Each one of you has intuition. You are born with it. As children you followed your gut instincts frequently but as you matured, your rational mind taught you to ignore intuition.

Some call it divine intelligence and I have relied on my intuition several times in my life. I have to trust in God's guidance every time I enter into the space of helping others heal, and also in my coaching and training. As a result, I have developed a keen sense of intuition. I now trust, as I know that divine intelligence is always available and willing to lovingly guide me. Everyone has the ability to receive guidance through intuition and the more you develop it, the easier it gets, until it becomes second nature. You just have to listen and trust.

I like to call it my sixth sense because it goes beyond our senses of taste, hearing, touch, smell, and sight. Intuitive messages bombard us every day. It is just a matter of whether or not we listen to them. By following through on our everyday hunches, we are actually honing in on our intuitive listening skills. The more we use our intuition, the better we become at hearing it. When we listen to our intuition, it connects us with a greater knowledge and can act as a valuable guide as we move toward creating the life we desire. Intuition is our ability to acquire knowledge without the process of rational thought.

Reason. Reason is your ability to think, use logic, gather information, and make decisions.

Ultimately, it's the mental process where you look for reasons, beliefs, conclusions, actions or feelings. The majority of young children don't have the ability to choose for themselves the thoughts, beliefs, or ideas they will accept into their subconscious mind because their intellectual faculty of reason hasn't developed yet. Until a child reaches about 8 years old, everything that comes in goes in, and stays in, and ultimately becomes their self-image.

You are granted the ability to think and to reason, but the majority of people aren't aware that this ability exists. If you don't know something is there, how are you supposed to figure out how to use it? One way is your internal private eye gathering clues and information from the world around you, relating it to past memories and experiences, and then putting it all together to make sense of the situation.

Because you are not taught about your faculty of reason and how to use it, more than likely you spend most of your time on autopilot. This is exactly what happened to me. I did not even know that I had this faculty. I lived in a space of ignorance. The pain of life's adversities helped me to discover that I have the power to think, to reason. As I started to understand this concept, I decided to take it seriously and look at my life to identify the areas where I was not getting the results that I wanted. I knew I had carelessly accepted beliefs, ideas and messages that were not empowering my life. I knew I had to take control of my thinking, so I used affirmations to let go of the limiting language or thoughts that I accepted in my conscious mind without thinking. I also took a look at the TV programs I watched and noticed how they adversely impacted me. As a result, I stopped watching the news, violent movies and all negative programs. I also reviewed radio programs and written media and one by one, I eliminated them from my life. I went as far as paying attention to the song's lyrics of my music and although I liked them, I decided to do a cleansing. I also made a conscious decision to listen to what people had to say and without going into arguments, responsibly accept only what resonated with the truth of my being. I came to the realization that it was I who was in charge of the garden of my heart and I now take full responsibility for what I plant in it. When I purged all of the negativity from my life, I experienced an awakening. Just like me, you too also have a choice, moment to moment, to exercise your faculty of reason, and to create your heaven here on earth by what you cultivate in your mind.

Fully utilizing your faculty of reason gives you the power of discernment to not go with the flow, blend with the crowd or follow the masses. You will be in a position of not having to accept

the general way of thinking, speaking and acting of those around you. If you want to live your absolute best life, you have to first have a clear picture of your mind, learn how it operates and take advantage of all of the wonderful intellectual faculties stored deep inside. Learning more about your mind and how to exercise its mental muscles throughout your daily activities can literally change your life. Use the power of your intellectual faculties to make conscious choices to help you become a success.

— *Glorious Discovery* —

- Make a list of the weeds in your subconscious mind and clear them out by replacing them with positive buds of thought. Remove all negative phrases, sayings or expressions. Think of sentences that are opposite and create affirmations.

- Now that you understand the mind, you have the power to choose which thoughts enter your subconscious mind. Choose well.

- Observe yourself and be committed to only accepting into your conscious mind the ideas or beliefs that will empower you.

- Make it a daily habit to use affirmations to replace any negative thoughts or language in any area of your life. Affirmations are positive statements expressed in the present time. For example, *It's a Beautiful Day. I create it with the power of my mind.*

- Take responsibility for the events in your life by paying attention to the decisions you make moment to moment.

- Think on a Higher Level. Work around any type of circumstance by removing what does not serve you and by staying positive.

- Review the Intellectual Faculties and make a list of how you can apply them to improve your results.

· Imagination: Give yourself permission to dream. Use the power of your imagination to create your life. Have a clear picture of what you desire and allow it to come into your life by trusting your Creator who is in charge of the how. Receive it by imagining that you already have what you desire.

· Will: Make the commitment to use this faculty to accomplish what you want. Set up the intention and give it your very best.

· Perception: Choose to see the positive aspects of each experience and to view the world as if you are living in heaven.

· Memory: Affirm that you have perfect memory and you affirmation will become your reality. Consciously exercise your memory in all situations.

· Intuition: Learn to follow and trust your internal guidance. It has all the answers that you need to make wise decisions. The more you rely on it the more it will show you its treasures and will guide you to create a successful life.

· Reason: Using this powerful faculty you can be selective of the thoughts you accept in your conscious mind, the language that you speak and your actions. Using this faculty responsibly determines the quality of your life.

Affirm:

- I use the power of my *Imagination* to create what I want

- I am committed to use my *will* to accomplish my heart's desires

- I use my faculty of *perception* to see the positive aspects of each experience

- I develop my mental faculty of *memory* with joy and ease

- I use my *intuition* to guide me in creating a successful life

- I exercise my faculty of *reason* to make successful decisions

Chapter 4

Believe in Yourself and Thrive

Several years ago, I took stock of myself and realized that my thoughts created my life. Rather than having a life of happiness and abundance, I lived life in denial by pretending that everything was perfect. After my second divorce, I soon realized that I couldn't control anyone but myself. When I learned to control my thoughts, I began to enjoy life the way it was meant to be enjoyed. We are put here to enjoy life and live it to the fullest. Whatever we experience in our life is totally connected to our thoughts. Our thoughts create our reality.

Before I understood the importance of thoughts and learned to understand the mind, I reacted instead of responding. I reacted not only to my husband but also to anyone I had a significant relationship with. In my reactive state, I never once tried to make sense of anything they did; instead, I made assumptions and accusations that didn't make any sense. For instance, many times in my second marriage, my husband told me that I made up accusations and I in turn argued that he was wrong because I was certain of my thoughts. No matter how hard he tried, he couldn't change my mind. I blamed him for doing things that hadn't even entered his mind. I did not give him the chance to explain himself. This kind of behavior comes from insecurity and low self-esteem, which is why it is so important to pay attention to your behavior and be committed to believing in yourself. Reacting is out of anger and criticism. Responding comes from using our faculty of reason. When you respond, you let go and allow God to guide you to handle the event or circumstance in a peaceful and loving way.

I learned to respond instead of react. In addition, I also learned to use my reasoning mind to behave in a way that is self-loving to myself and to others. Now I am able to surrender to God and let go. A student in one of my classes called me one day very upset that someone was talking badly about me. I told her that I didn't want to know who this person was or what they were saying about me. I explained to her that she needed to let go and not allow her heart to be contaminated with negative feelings. I then asked her to pray with me about this other person and after about fifteen minutes she understood the power of forgiveness and letting go and I never heard of this situation again.

When you are in the picture you can't see the frame, and that is why I always ask people to seek help, because you don't even realize that you keep doing the same things over and over again, expecting different results. That is the definition of insanity. I am so grateful to Al-Anon and the help they gave me to overcome my long held subconscious thoughts. When you are able to control your perception and thoughts, you can then control your emotions and respond rather than react. I took control of my thoughts, eliminated fear and confronted the obstacles in my life, which transformed me from a victim to a victor. Each day, tell yourself that you believe in yourself and you'll thrive.

A True Understanding

A favorite quote of mine by Edward de Bono is, "Intelligence is something we are born with. Thinking is a skill that must be learned." These words speak volumes to me. You can be the smartest person in the room and still be the unhappiest. Intelligence doesn't equate with fulfillment. When people don't have any understanding of how their thoughts affect their lives, they spend their days on a rollercoaster. One day they are up and happy and the next day they are at rock bottom because they are basing their emotions on external factors rather than internal ones. How many of you enjoy your work one day and the next day you hate it? Or one day you get along with your spouse and the next day you don't? That is the rollercoaster that I am talking about.

The same holds true for your finances, one day you can buy gas and the next day you don't have money for gas. This is what happens when you live in the space of ignorance instead of understanding. This is also a life of bondage because you are held back by your ignorance. The good news is that you can change any of the above scenarios. A good example of a positive outcome through taking control of your thoughts is when my family visited me a couple of months ago. They made plans to go shopping and come back in a couple of hours to pick me up to go to lunch. I wanted to spend time with them but I had a tight schedule with clients. They showed up an hour late and instead of me being upset, I had already come up with plan B, which they totally loved and everyone was happy. I used my reasoning power and handled the situation with easy and joy.

I have to continuously train myself to make the choice to respond instead of react. You have a choice to control your thoughts and consequently your behavior. Don't get into the frame of mind that you do not have a choice. To be able to learn to respond to life situations with peace and joy, you have to be willing to let go of the old aspects of you that don't serve you well and replace them with life-winning habits. You have to embrace change. The majority of people who come to me for help admit that they don't like change. After talking with them, more often than not, I discover that they have tried to change their entire life or thought process in a day and expect the change to be instant and forever. Have you ever said that you are going to get out of a set of specific circumstances and get the books and the knowledge that it takes to move yourself forward from a life of bondage only to return to the same way of living? Change is a process and takes time on your part. It doesn't happen overnight. It takes effort, diligence, patience and discipline to take control and get rid of the negative thoughts. The process of change is one step at a time made with a willful desire using the God given power you already possess. More than likely your real dread is not change, but rather the process of change.

One of the primary reasons so many people don't change their thoughts is that they don't know where they originated from. If you go back and look at the image of the mind in the previous chapter, you'll notice that your thoughts come into your conscious mind from all sorts of outside sources, and you can choose to accept or reject them. Once thoughts or ideas are accepted by your conscious mind, your subconscious mind takes them as facts because it does not have the power to reject them. As a child, I'm sure you heard all sorts of different kinds of comments that for one reason or another got stuck in your subconscious mind. These remarks or opinions of others weren't filtered by your reasoning ability, and as a result you weren't able to sort through it and keep what you wanted and get rid of what you didn't. The majority of times, the words of your parents, teachers and other influential people become old tapes that repeat on a continuous loop in your mind. These opinions don't serve you anymore. They are false. Do the opinions and words of others dictate your life? If the answer is yes, then you are living according to inaccurate paradigms or outdated beliefs.

Many times these beliefs have been passed down from generation to generation. When I was a child, for example, I was constantly told to be careful of this or careful of that or you'll get hurt; so that by the time I was an adult, I had this fear ingrained into me. When you rid your life of these outdated limiting beliefs, you can elevate yourself to a higher plane. I grew up very poor and struggled with the belief that I could not afford an abundant living. Now, whenever I go to buy something I have an attitude of prosperity and I tell myself that I am the child of a very rich father. I think that every single day you have to work on shifting any negative beliefs and embrace a mentality of prosperity.

My many years of coaching and working with people from across the globe have helped me understand that the biggest paradigm or belief that is passed down from generation to generation is the idea of our imperfection, that we are not good enough. This is a false idea based on pure ignorance and it is crucial that we remove it from our conscious mind and don't continue passing it down from generation to generation. You are good enough and can do anything you put your mind to. God created you to live a life of happiness. You are designed to be, have and do whatever you desire. In addition to the idea that they aren't good enough, many people don't believe in a higher power. This is one of the most serious beliefs you can have. If you think you're just here and do not have any reverence for a higher power you won't have reverence for anything. The best gift you can give to yourself is to consciously connect and develop a relationship with your Creator on a daily basis.

With God there are no limitations, He is pure abundance. I think about it like a waterfall, which never questions if there is enough water. The water keeps coming and it never worries about where it is coming from or questions that it will not come. It is absolutely the same thing with a human being; God's abundance is there for us and it is our responsibility to accept it without questioning or doubting that it is. Nature is a living demonstration of the abundance of the universe. As you trust and continue to share your abundance, doors will open for you because you have shifted your consciousness.

Handle Every Situation in Your Life with Ease and Joy

I am grateful today that the challenging experiences I have faced in my life triggered me to look for a better answer than what had been going on in my life. As I walked through the garden of my thoughts, I soon realized that my attitude played a large role in how I felt. I love a quote by Henry Ford. He said, "If you think you can, or you think you can't – either way you are right." You have the ability to decide your own results! It starts with your attitude. How many times have you heard, "Be careful of what you wish for, because you just might get it?" The types of words that make up your vocabulary are representative of your attitude. Do you constantly say "I can't" or "I don't"? During difficult times, I've heard people say, "What more can happen" and then all of a sudden something else bad occurs. Why? Because they literally asked for it. When you throw your arms up in the air out of frustration and wonder what bad thing or situation is going to happen next, guess what, the universe is going to give you exactly what you asked for!

Your attitude is a powerful and creative force that allows you to have the life you've been dreaming of. The thoughts you align your attitude with will manifest into your reality. For example, if your attitude is focused on gaining new clients and growing your business, your winning behavior will attract positive situations. Why? Because your entire focus is on abundance and prosperity rather than on lack and loss. Attitude is the composition of thoughts, words, feelings and actions. Now realize this can go either way, positive or negative. You can achieve anything by having a good attitude. Attitude is the feeling of gratitude, love, and joy. Having the right attitude in life is really the most important thing that you can do.

Your thoughts and attitudes can come from many different sources including the media, your family and friends, and even yourself. Since the thoughts you receive in your conscious mind become feelings, it makes perfect sense to become more aware of what you think. Become vigilant and pay attention to your thoughts and feelings. If you feel happy, happy thoughts are entering your mind. Commit to fostering positive thoughts. They will lead you to positive feelings and this vibration will propel your entire body to take positive actions. It is like a ripple effect. That's why you must become responsible for your thoughts and feelings. When you get up in the morning and you have beautiful thoughts, these thoughts will translate into a beautiful day and you will have a wonderful day.

Feel confident that you can make progress every day to become more conscious of the power of your thoughts. This is how you believe in yourself to thrive. Consider putting into practice these ideas mentioned below to renew your mind to thrive:

- **Find help and take action.** Everyone knows someone who is wounded and needs help. For me it was the 12 steps, a spiritual awakening program originally created by AA. For you it could be a book, a seminar, a mentor. I love Les Brown's quote, "When you are in the picture you cannot see the frame." Working with a mentor or a coach can help you understand what are the changes that you need to make to move in the right direction. This takes humbleness. You have to let go of the EGO (edging God out). It has been said that "most people don't participate in their own rescue." Take action. "The price of greatness is responsibility." Winston Churchill

- **Align yourself with like-minded people who are on the path to transforming their lives.** This way you are challenged to excel. They will hold you to higher standards. This has been my experience as part of Les Brown's Platinum Speakers Network. My association with them has stretched me to the level of soaring with eagles, to really tapping into my God-given talents and gifts. Be motivated to stretch yourself and continue to learn and expand your horizons.

- **Find your purpose, your reason for being here.** Your heart's desires are your road map to your purpose. Follow them with faith and determination. Once you are clear about your purpose, master it. Your heart's desires were placed there for a reason, to fulfill them.

How do you see yourself 3-5 years from now? Visualize yourself accomplishing your dreams. Go ask people who know you best 3-4 things they most like about you. Experiment with your life. There are 2 important questions you must ask yourself:

1. Where am I going?

2. Who is going with me?

You have to get them in the right order. After I invested several years healing my past, forgiving people and purifying my heart, the doors opened up for me in magical ways. The teachers, mentors, classes and books started to show up in perfect sequence. I was conscious of the divine order in operation and how it was taking me in the direction of my mission. My life took an amazing turn into the field of personal development. At first I was very scared and doubtful that I was taking the right path. The support of mentors and other teachings helped me to trust in my new path. As I got more comfortable every day, I ventured into new things and these new experiences gave me more faith and certainty that I was moving in the direction of my reason for being here. Today, I feel grateful and happy to be living God's calling for me. As the clarity is revealed to me about where I am going, I move with faith and determination. As I am guided to the people that are going with me, I embrace them. This is what I call "living life guided by the Spirit of God."

You also have the opportunity to embrace your calling in this lifetime. All you have to do is be willing to allow the Creator to show you the way. Remember, "God is in charge of the how." He will show you where to go and with whom. You just have to trust the journey and every day a little more will be revealed to you. As you continue to believe in yourself, you will thrive in all areas of your life.

— Glorious Discovery —

- Repetition is the key to changing outdated beliefs.

- Read positive books, listen to encouraging messages or programs that reinforce your new beliefs.

- Connect with your Creator.

  · Find a verse from a holy book.

  · Meditate on that verse for 15 minutes a day.

  · Look for the deeper meaning or understanding of that verse during your meditation.

  · Journal your meditation session.

  · Thank the Creator.

- Create an affirmation sheet.

  Write down on your affirmation sheet what it is that you want to accomplish, no matter what, and reread it often until it becomes your new paradigm.

- Gratitude List.

  Write down a gratitude list every day giving thanks for all your blessings. This is a very powerful way to keep your abundance flowing. Start your list with, I am grateful for ...

Affirm:

- I believe in myself and thrive
- I handle each life situation with ease and joy
- I respond to my experiences with peace and understanding
- I align myself with successful people
- I live in an abundant universe

Chapter 5

Forgive and Be Free

One of the primary challenges many people encounter when they attempt to move forward in life is forgiveness. In fact, some never quite gain the ability to forgive. Forgiveness seems so foreign doesn't it? If you "forgive" those people who have wronged you, do you "forget" about what they did? How can you? Won't they just do it again? These are examples and questions that often have no easy answers, and this chapter combined with my own journey of forgiveness will hopefully shed some light on its importance.

Before I go any further in this chapter, let me first define what forgiveness means to me – the ability to let go completely. So many people have a difficult time with the idea of letting go because to them that means they have to let a betrayal or hurt go unpunished. Now please don't misunderstand me, unjust deeds are just that – unjust. True forgiveness liberates you by giving you the courage to release all of the negative emotions associated with a certain act or deed. If someone speaks harshly or crudely to you, it is imperative to tell them straight away that when they are ready to act respectfully, you will sit down and talk with them.

Sometimes, you may have a difficult time offering forgiveness because you are the one at fault. I know for me, when I experienced difficulty with forgiveness, I needed to sit down and have a stern talk with myself. If, for instance, someone was disrespectful toward me maybe it was because I disrespected them. Each issue you experience with another human is really nothing more than a mirror. Whenever challenges arise with someone in your life, you have to look inside of yourself to see what you need to change on the inside before you start to throw rocks at the other person. There is a wonderful book entitled *A Course in Miracles.* Its principle message is that "there is nothing to forgive" because forgiveness is all about perception. I embraced this concept and am now a self-proclaimed master forgiver. I can honestly say that I no longer have issues with forgiveness. If I should have an issue with someone I quickly remedy the situation by forgiving them within 24 hours. That is exactly the rule that I practice. I used to get upset very easily and had the reputation in my family for reacting to situations. In the process, I hurt people's feelings. I now respond to situations by not taking anything personally and thinking before I speak. The person who needed to change was me.

Open Your Mind and Your Heart

The first time I read *A Course in Miracles*, I had a difficult time understanding the concept that there is nothing to forgive because forgiveness is all about our perceptions. This is profound because people have to be reminded that there is nothing to forgive. You have to be open-minded and for many years I wasn't. I lived each day with a mind sealed shut by the strongest metal lock ever made. For many years I close-mindedly believed that the people who hurt me needed to be punished. I punished them by gossiping and doing hurtful things to them. I didn't realize that I was doing all of these things to myself.

When you don't forgive others you are taking poison and expecting them to die. People that tried to teach me to forgive were met with feelings of resentment. I lived by the philosophy that forgiveness was impossible for me. I couldn't forgive anybody for anything. When I was in this state of mind it affected my finances, relationships with others and every aspect of my life. It even affected my health. I lived in ignorance. I carried around so much hurt that my shoulders were sore. I was so bogged down by pain and anguish that I couldn't move forward. Instead, I lived in the past. Each day I got out of bed, I took one step forward and two steps backward into my emotional baggage. My second divorce forced me to consider seeking counsel from both a mentor and a higher power. My mentor helped me to understand that I needed to change from the inside out. As I continued to let go of resentments, my relationship with my Higher Power grew stronger.

As long as we hold onto the pain, we allow someone else's past actions to continue to hurt us. Forgiveness empowers us to stop letting people dictate our emotions. I've worked very hard to change my belief system so I can forgive unconditionally. Several years ago when I struggled with forgiveness, my mentor suggested that I work on a powerful forgiveness process called "Review of Resentments" and to write three columns on a single page. The first column was for the people I was willing to forgive. The second column was for the people I was not sure I wanted to forgive and the third column was for the people I had no intention to forgive. In the third column I included my Dad, my step-mother and my brother-in-law. My mentor explained that I shouldn't worry about the second and third columns. As I reviewed the list of people in my last column, I felt I was never going to forgive the people I included.

For each person I listed in the first column, my mentor asked me to answer the following questions:

- What did they do to cause my anger? I had to express my anger toward these people on paper. I burned the paper once I did it.

- How their behavior affected me?

- What was my part in this experience? (Did I hold onto resentment or criticize the person or punish them in any way?)

When I finished the process for each person in the first column, I moved on to the list of people in column two. And to my surprised, after I was done with the second list, I felt so good that I decided to tackle the most difficult one, column three.

Once I completed the "Review of Resentments", I proceeded to work on my "Review of Amends" which required me to list the people I knew I had hurt, willingly or indirectly because of my actions. After I made my list, I had to write down how I hurt them, how it made me feel and my reason for not asking for forgiveness. Once I finished my list, I contacted them by phone, e-mail or letter and apologized for my wrongdoing. In this step, you do not have to get into the details; just let them know that you want to heal your heart. If the person is no longer alive you can still write and when you finish you can place the letter in a sacred book.

Embracing forgiveness filled me with genuine compassion. Overcome with a great feeling of relief, I received a real rush of gratitude and blessings from being willing to have an impeccable heart. Each column cleansed my heart and healed my soul. After I found forgiveness in my heart, I soon realized that holding on to past hurts affected my leadership and all those people around me. My finances suffered from lack of forgiveness, and once I forgave the people listed in my columns, my life became much easier, which allowed me to redirect the wasted energy I used on grudges toward prosperity. After I found forgiveness, I no longer lived in ignorance.

My mind and heart are now free to create loving and positive experiences. I live with peace and appreciate others' differences. I've kept my promise ever since I made those three columns and have continuously forgiven those who offended me. I have either called the person, or wrote about it, or during my meditation time I speak to them in the spirit and let go of whatever it was that had caused me to think harshly about them.

To enjoy the benefits of forgiveness, the "Review of Resentments" and "Review of Amends" is a must for anyone who struggles with hurt. When you have a clear and impeccable heart, God is able to use you to do what needs to be done. God has been able to use my life and me in many incredible ways and I don't live in turmoil any more. Make the decision to move forward in forgiveness rather than backward in betrayal.

Radical Forgiveness

Forgiveness was instrumental in helping me heal the pain of going through my divorce. Forgiveness means that you're committed to moving on. It means that you realize that you have a choice to let go of the resentments and choose love. When people tell me that they are unable to forgive, then one of three things can be happening. Either the person doesn't understand that forgiveness is more for them than the person who hurt them (as you can't really move forward if you hold on to pain and negativity); or the person needs to process their emotions; or the person has not received or asked for what they need in order to offer this forgiveness in a healthy and genuine way.

If you're at a point where you cannot yet think about forgiving, then ask yourself what you need that you are not getting. If this is something that you need from the other person, then have the courage to ask them for it. Whether this is reassurance, information, affection, or working through issues or doubts, it's very unlikely that you will be able to genuinely offer your forgiveness once you get these things. And, you deserve them as much as anyone else does and you can have it through the radical forgiveness process.

I am a person that is extremely patient with my clients and people that come to my classes and my conferences. I do not judge people and I tend to demonstrate compassion to help them heal their hearts. I always say that my approach is like using a white glove. I tell my clients that it is possible to forgive through love even if you don't understand it. I tell them about the changes that will come and how much better they will feel if they just do their best to forgive from a standpoint of love. I always see amazing miracles because people are willing to do it one step at a time. I had one client who had issues with her sister who owed her a lot of money. She was willing to let go and during one session she let go of a lot grief and anger. During the next week her sister sent her a check for sixty thousand dollars. This was a result of her willingness to forgive. She went through the process of radical forgiveness and of course the results were amazing.

Another example of radical forgiveness was a client of mine. On more than one occasion, she shared her experiences with me about her interaction with men. I told her that this was most likely because of her father and she had to forgive him. She argued that her relationships with men had nothing to do with her father. Years later she decided to do my twelve steps to mastery coaching program and when she got to the forgiveness step, I helped her work through it. We worked through radical forgiveness by sitting down to complete a three-step process. This process is done once you complete the "Review of Resentments" for each person on the three-column list. The first step allowed her to let out all of her emotions. In the second step, she wrote a list of the behaviors she did not like about her father. Then she looked within herself to see if she had the same behaviors. People are mirrors for us of what we need to change within ourselves. Sure enough, maybe not at the same level of intensity, she realized that her father was a mirror of what needed to change in her. In the third letter she took the list of negative behaviors and found a quality for each one. This was the list of new qualities that she was now committing to demonstrating in her life every day.

She decided to go and see her father to share what she had discovered in this process. It turned out to be a beautiful sharing weekend with him. She told him about the letters and he also shared aspects of his life with her. The healing they both experienced was powerful. She came back and was so happy that she had resolved the issues with her dad. Three weeks later she received a phone call that her father had died unexpectedly. Later she was the co-author in the book, *Why You Still Need to Forgive Your Parents*, where she wrote about her experience, as this was really a moving story. She was extremely happy that she had taken the steps she did.

If you are having a difficult time and you work through it, you will go to the top of the mark. You have to be willing to do the work and be glad you did it. Lack of forgiveness affects all areas of your life, including your health. Research illustrates that cancer is caused by lack of forgiveness. Lack of forgiveness causes your emotions to eat up your body and that is usually manifested by cancer. I wrote this book to help others overcome challenges, obstacles and outright trauma. I wouldn't have been able to help anyone had it not been for my own experience with forgiveness.

I know some of you who read this chapter may still not be convinced that forgiveness is possible. A few may have to re-read this chapter several times to gain an understanding of the importance of forgiveness. I encourage you to always be motivated to forgive and forget the wrongs done to you by others, based upon God's love, not based upon whether the person has earned or deserves your forgiveness. Truth be told, forgiveness takes some work, but with the help of your Higher Power and an open mind, you can forgive anyone for anything. Greater things are just ahead for those who learn the art of forgiving.

— Glorious Discovery —

1. Think about the people in your life who have hurt you and do the following:

   "Review of Resentments" - On a single page, make three columns.

A. In the first column write down the names of people you are willing to forgive. In the second column write down the names of people you aren't sure you want to forgive. In the third column, write down the names of people you have no intention of forgiving.

B. Start with the people in the first column and answer the following questions:

   · What did they do to cause my anger? Express your anger toward these people on paper. Destroy the paper once you do it.

   · How their behavior affected me?

   · What was my part my part on this experience? (Did I hold onto resentment or criticize the person or punish them in any way?)

C. Do the same with the people in the second and third column

2. The Radical Forgiveness Process

A. Express your feelings in writing about each person on your list

B. Write a list of the behaviors you dislike like about each person on your list.

Then look within yourself to see if you had the same behaviors. People are mirrors for us of what we need to change within ourselves.

Take the list of negative behaviors and find a quality for each one. This is the list of new qualities that now you must commit to demonstrating in your life every day. Write an affirmation for each quality.

C. Thank the person for being a teacher to help you heal the behaviors that you spotted on yourself. End the exercise with a positive statement. I fully and freely forgive you.

3. Think about the people in your life that you have hurt willingly or indirectly because of your actions and complete the "Review of Amends"

A. Write down the names of people you have hurt, willingly or indirectly because of your actions.

B. Next to each name, write down how you hurt them, how it made you feel and your reason for not asking forgiveness.

C. Contact the people on your list and apologize for your wrongdoing. Remember, you don't have to go into specific details, just apologize and let them know you want to heal your heart. If the person is no longer alive, you can still write and when you finish you can place the letter in a sacred book.

Affirm:

- I forgive because I love myself so much
- I keep my heart pure
- Forgiveness is my doorway to freedom
- I see divine order in every life experience
- I forgive and my heart blossoms

Chapter 6

Learn to Love Yourself

I would not be where I am today if it weren't for two important lessons my life experiences taught me. The first one we discussed in the previous chapter – forgiveness. I worked extremely hard to forgive those who hurt me, yet I still clung to some destructive emotions and continued to think of myself as a victim. I desperately wanted to move forward and live as a victor. After some deep soul searching, I had a spiritual epiphany in which I realized that forgiveness was only part of the equation. I had to learn to love too. Forgiveness only opened the door for me to learn about the importance of love.

I loved my two husbands, but it wasn't true love. My attitude about love was completely skewed. I used to think to myself, "When you do this for me, I'll do that for you." My love for them was conditional. As a matter of fact, my love for everyone in my life was conditional. I was only interested in what they could do for me. If I didn't get what I wanted, I was sarcastic and hurt them. Angry at myself, I unconsciously reacted at people by getting upset. I expected them to act according to my needs, not their own. I was selfish.

I couldn't love my husbands or anyone else for that matter because I didn't even love myself. When we don't have love in our being we are jealous and testy and out of alignment. For so many years, resentment, anger, shame and regret kept me focused on the past and blocked me from accessing true love. Love has caused such an amazing transformation in my life. I believe we are spirit and spirit is pure unconditional love. Love allowed me to release the anger and pain. It gave me the strength to live in the present rather than the past. I don't ever think anymore about what happened. I have been able to release all of my painful emotions from my childhood and move on. Once we're able to experience true unconditional self-love, we've received one of the greatest keys to aligning with our true essence and making positive and lasting changes in our life. When we are able to live in love, our lives become more meaningful. Love is truly one of the best gifts we can ever give to ourselves.

The Greatest Love of All

We often tend to think of love as an emotion or an expression, but it is so much more. Love is unconditional, accepting, inclusive, uniting, understanding, kind and joining. It's a freedom from fear and separateness. It's about showing compassion and kindness to not only ourselves but to the world around us. It's also a commitment to reduce suffering as we respect God's creation. His essence is the greatest love of all. His love flows through every living being, connecting us to one another, the living planet, and the Divine. His love sustains the universe. He made us in His image and likeness. It's our responsibility to share His love with others including our enemies. Love is at the very essence of who we are.

We are extensions of God and this is why we are capable of doing great things, if we believe. Mother Theresa, for instance, knew that God would show her the way and she lived her life according to His will of loving and serving others. As we allow God to show us the way, our lives become purpose-driven. For many years of my life, I didn't live according to my essence and followed my path instead of God's. Before my mother died, she was able to teach me about the essence of God. But after she died, I fell into a deep state of despair and fell victim to my stepmother's words. She constantly reminded my brothers and I how bad we were and how we kept her from a happy life with my father. She had no patience or love for us. She wanted us out of the house. She did such a good job of convincing us that we were ignorant and no good.

When I became an adult I had no clue that God lived inside of me. I was unhappy and looking for happiness outside of me. I grew up as a Catholic and I believed that God lived in the heavens above and was a very punishing God. I had no idea that God was a loving God and was present everywhere including inside of me. Without this understanding, one day I would be up and the next day I would be down expecting people to make me happy. I absolutely had no idea of what was going on with me because I didn't have a close relationship with God.

By the time I went through my second divorce I decided that I didn't want to have another marriage that would possibly end in divorce. It felt like I was living a lie and that happiness would never be a reality for me. I knew I needed help. When you are in the picture you cannot see the frame. For many, many years, I couldn't see that I needed to change from the inside. I finally decided to look at myself with the help of coaches, mentors, seminars, books, reading and studying. When I was thirty-nine years old, I finally discovered that my body was the extension of God and His Spirit lived inside me. For the first time in my life, I went from living in the dark to living in the light.

Our essence defines us as spiritual beings because it originates from the spirit of God. We have been conditioned to believe that we are our bodies and in all actuality we are really spirit and the essence of God is in us. When we are in alignment with God we're not going to do anything that will hurt another person. If we have love we won't hurt anyone and we don't have to have them do anything for us. We accept them the way they are. Not wanting to change people is true freedom. The focus is on me, to be the best human being I can be. If I am at peace with my creator and live according to His laws, I will always be truly successful.

If you are in alignment with your creator you will be obedient to His guidance and will for you. In the year 2004 my coach suggested for me to start a not-for-profit organization. I did not know the reason why. However, I was willing to be obedient. I asked for a sign from God and sure enough, I got it the next day. I went to a networking meeting where I met a lady who handed me a business card. She told me she specialized in helping people put together not-for-profits. I started working with her and in a few months the IRS approved my organization as a 501 (c)(3).

God's essence is in every cell of our bodies. It is not physical or conjugal. It exists in all our parts. If the body dies our essence continues on as pure spirit. We are eternal in spirit. Once we leave this earth, our spirit of love, compassion and joy lives on and because of that our essence never dies. I invite you to express the light of love in everything you think, say, and do. Commit to sharing "agape love" - unconditional love, with everyone in your life and yourself. The rewards are a happy, healthy and prosperous life.

Unconditional Love

While our ego minds tend to analyze, think, and judge, our hearts immerse us in love. I know love, for some, may seem like one of those intangible ideals that's just out of reach or a waste of time. But it's not. Just like I did, you too can find love. And by making that decision, you can move forward on your path. It is not possible to have unconditional love for anyone, including yourself, when your life is not centered on the love of God. I was centered in the paradigms that were given to me when I was growing up. My conditioning of the past, including fear not feeling good enough, anger and control, were blocking the flow of love.

Unconditional love means that we respect each other no matter what their perception of life is. We love each other despite our differences.

People who understand their essence seem to love unconditionally because they see the true essence in others. They know that other people have different ideas and perceptions and they don't get intimidated by the opinions or behaviors of others. They are centered in their essence. Unconditional love is the ability to see the real essence of a person and not the appearances. They realize others don't always see things the same way they do, as the other person may have their own viewpoint, but they have the ability to adjust and work through their differences.

The first half of my life I lived without having any idea of my essence or love. The love that I learned is that if you do it for me you love me, but if you don't do it you don't love me. I lived according to conditional love. This way of living wreaked havoc on my self-esteem. I didn't love myself at all. I didn't have self-confidence and wasn't able to stand up for myself. As a result, I endured emotional and sometimes verbal abuse from people. I went through some terrible times when I had low self-esteem and when I learned more about myself I decided that I never, ever wanted to go back to that time again. I reclaimed my power.

Feeling worthy requires you to see yourself with fresh eyes of self-awareness and love. Acceptance and love must come from within. Each of us has a unique belief system, a way of seeing the world that is slightly different to everyone else's. It's almost like our perception and belief system has a fingerprint. What turns us on, what turns us off? What we feel is important. If you feel like love is impossible, look at your upbringing and beliefs and then compare them with the repeating patterns in your life. When you don't know how to love, the same hurts find ways of showing up again and again. If you still feel like you're a victim of something, you remain attached to that experience and it becomes part of your identity. You can rise above pain and see that everything has a purpose for rich lessons. When you accept your life as perfect just the way it is, love shows you the way and you're able to fully immerse yourself in life.

Anyone in a relationship must come to realize how crucial it is to understand the importance of unconditional love. Many couples I've counseled, whether it is the husband or the wife, want to have the other person see the world with their perception. They put conditions on their partners. Many of the couples want the other to conform to their beliefs and perceptions. This behavior is in direct opposition with unconditional love. I explain that if they start arguing they have to stop right away, otherwise it can escalate into a big fight. They can find the time to journal their feelings and release their anger first and then sit down and talk. I emphasize on the importance of respect in relationships.

I invite them to have "heart to heart" conversations, which means that one person talks first. Once he/she finishes, then the other person expresses his/her feelings. This way they don't interrupt each other and instead truly listen to each other. I explain to them that they both are bringing limiting conditioning from their childhood and this is an opportunity to heal the wounds of the past so they don't keep repeating the same behaviors. After they express their feelings, respectfully, they discuss the possible solutions. Once they have agreed on the solutions, they write agreements so they know what to expect from their commitment. These agreements always have amazing results in couples, families, and partners.

Once a couple is centered in unconditional love, their individual selves flourish as well as their relationship. Love is the catalyst of well-being. It is our responsibility to live our lives in love to be able to experience a fulfilling life. That love is the love that comes from within and it is inexhaustible. It continues to give. It means that we were created in the image and likeness of God and the image of God is pure love. Love is the essence of spirit and we are reminded everyday that love is the way we can achieve what we want to do, be or have.

Once we understand that God's love is in us, we have an inner goodness and a desire to share ourselves with the world. Loving our essence isn't a one time event. It's an endless, moment-by-moment ongoing process. Love begins with us unfolding ourselves in our affection and appreciation. The most important decision of your life, the one that will affect every other decision you make, is the commitment to love and accept yourself. Unconditional love directly affects the quality of your relationships, work, free time, faith, and your future.

You are worthy of love. Together, through our love, we can heal each other, the world, and ourselves. Love is your purpose, your true calling. It begins with and *within* each of us. You are love. You are a beautiful creation of God. You are a glorious loving being. Live each day in the magnificence of genuine unconditional love.

— Glorious Discovery —

- Begin your day with love. Remind yourself of your worthiness before getting out of bed. Breathe in love and breathe out love. Enfold yourself in light. Saturate your being in love.

- Take time to mediate and journal. Spend time focusing inward daily. Begin with 5 minutes of meditation and 5 minutes of journaling each morning. Gradually increase this time.

- Let go of any anger and resentment. You can never see the whole picture. You don't know what anything is for. Stop fighting against yourself by thinking and desiring people and events in your life *should* be different. Your plan may be different from the creator's intentions.

- Work on personal and spiritual development. Be willing to surrender and grow. Life is a journey. We are here to learn and love on a deeper level.

- Own your potential. Love yourself enough to believe in the limitless opportunities available to you. Take action and create a beautiful life for yourself.

- Live in appreciation. Train your mind to be grateful. Appreciate your talents, beauty, and brilliance. You are a gift to the world.

Affirm:

- I love and accept myself exactly the way I am

- Love is the best gift I can give to others and myself

- I believe I am capable of doing great things

- I always do my best to embrace the limitless opportunities available to me

- I express the light of love in everything I think, say, and do

Chapter 7

Move Forward in Faith

For a very long time, I lived in bondage and was blind to the prison I had made for myself. I did not know that I was carrying my parent's habits and beliefs that were mostly based on fear and limitation. One of the biggest fears I grew up with was the fear of not having enough. This was a daily conversation in my home. I grew up with a distorted understanding of my real essence. My real self is courageous, not fearful. My parents' job was to help me stay aligned with the truth. Living with fear robs you of your happiness and the freedom to enjoy and be, have, or do whatever it is you desire. Fear prevents you from moving forward; it instead traps you into a state of an empty existence. **Fear destroys** your hopes and dreams and steals even the smallest joys.

Fear stems from every aspect of your life. Some people's fear stems from a relationship that went awry while others' fear surfaces whenever money is involved. Research shows that death is the number one fear humans have, followed by fear of speaking in public. The fear of death comes from not understanding that you never die because you are spirit, who is eternal. One of the biggest fears I had was public speaking. I was so shy that when people spoke to me I would feel my hands sweating and my face became red. I was afraid of what others would think of me. This was a fear based also on lack of understanding of my real essence, which is beautiful and powerful.

Out of this realization, I heard a little whisper that this is not what God wants me to experience in this lifetime. To conquer this fear, I worked on changing the conditions and paradigms I received as a child. I let go of any past hurts and told myself to replace all limiting beliefs with ideas of being capable of doing anything I wanted to do. I asked my Creator to help heal my old paradigms and get me into a position to change. I also worked with my inner child to help heal her wounds from childhood. This wasn't a quick process; it was instead a journey of transformation. A part of this transformation requires you to release any negative aspects of your past and replace your thoughts of inferiority with ones of empowerment. Along my journey, I made the decision to view myself as a good person who deserves respect. Once I changed my inner thoughts about myself, I expected only good to come to me rather than dwelling on fear of the future or dragging around experiences from the past. By changing your focus, the fear you're living in now doesn't have to control your future.

Look Inward

All negative emotions are rooted in fear. Fear manifests itself in several different forms ranging from anger to loneliness to insecurity to loss. At its mildest, fear surfaces as a feeling of discomfort or uneasiness. At its worst, fear prevents you from setting goals or following your dreams and can take you into depression if it is not controlled. Whenever you feel fearful, it is important to take a moment and ask yourself if the fear is justified or a reaction to a past event. There are specific issues that must be dealt with for any problem to change to a resolution. However, most think that if the external is changed the problem will no longer be there. That is only a surface band-aid that has roots that are deeper. To resolve a problem so it does not reoccur, the emotional energy from a number of areas must be addressed.

This is when you have to ask yourself to recall the messages you've heard or the behaviors you saw from the adults in your life while growing up that were based on fear. For each one of you the experience was different; however, the underlying message was the same: To fear people, situations, life, taking risks, or not having enough or trusting an infinite power. What is most important to know is that these behaviors have been passed down from generation to generation and it is time for us to stop it with you. You have the power to not accept any beliefs or behaviors based on fear. You have to make the decision right now to end it with your generation.

Many times, your perspective causes fear to multiply and grow out of control. My fear of feeling worthless cost me dearly. I questioned everything people said to me and allowed my twisted perception to turn their words against me. I felt inadequate and I assumed people thought I wasn't good enough to deserve their love. Whatever the root cause of your fear is, you need to take immediate action to relieve this feeling as otherwise it will remain a destructive and negative force in every area of your life. Your feelings in one area of life inevitably have an impact upon other areas of your life and color your experiences in general.

When I started working on myself I was accused of being self-centered. I didn't take the accusation personal because I believed that their words were actually a compliment. Why did I feel this way? Simple, because the more you align yourself with your Creator, the more self-confident you become. Some people find it difficult to accept the fact that you have improved yourself. The old saying "misery loves company" rings true in this situation. When you are unhappy and fearful, you have a common thread with those around who feel the same type of emotions. Once you look inward and make the decision to move forward in faith rather than fear, your friends and family who still live in bondage feel threatened or abandoned. As a result, this feeling of rejection manifests through other people accusing you of being self-centered.

An honest evaluation of ourselves can be difficult and many times people don't want to delve deep inside and see what resides in their beliefs. I knew I had to look inward to feel better. The information learned from mentors and all of the self-improvement books I read actually saved my life. I was trusting that the mentors were leading me in the right direction and I wanted to become more self-sufficient and learn more about myself and how to believe in myself. Today, I love and respect myself exactly the way I am. Sadly, those around me thought I felt superior. But that wasn't true, as my actions were a result of me loving my true self. A light shines through you when you truly love yourself. The glow of pure love we emit is obvious to others and they sense a change with you. When your self-esteem and self love increases, ,everything in life increases. For me, my health and finances improved and my relationships became more harmonious.

When people reach the space of losing everything to fear, it is time to take action. They need to change their lives by looking inward to find answers to their problems. Before any change can occur, you first have to be willing to take responsibility for what has happened and not dwell on the root cause experience; instead, transform the meaning of that root cause experience into something empowering. Sometimes you can't find the root cause because it is possible you haven't forgiven yourself. One of the first lessons I teach my clients is to forgive themselves. You need to release everything that is bothersome. When you forgive yourself, you're able to forget all of the past events and clear your mind enough to make an honest evaluation about the source of your fears. From a peaceful and forgiven place within yourself, first ask where the fear comes from. Once you find the answer, your next question is what action you must take to remove this belief.

By focusing on your fears, you will remain trapped in a downward spiral. Allowing yourself to remain in the mindset of "I can't cope" or "What if" makes you more insecure and paves the way to provide energy to attract that exact fear. In many instances, you have to identify the worst-case scenario to remove this fear. One way to do this is to face the fear. In my coaching I invite my clients to imagine the fear as a monster that is in the middle of their living room. It feels and looks quite scary and intimidating at the beginning and as you face it instead of hiding from it, you are able to diminish its power. I ask them to talk to it and to tell it that you are not going to be scared anymore because it's not real. Remember that FEAR is False Evidence Appearing Real. As you are willing to face the monster of fear, it loses its power and at last you are able to recover the power within yourself and open your heart to the unlimited possibilities that await you.

By confronting your original experience or experiences that started the fear, you can empower a change in your life. Think of this as "reprogramming the software" or as "deleting it from the hard drive". On occasion a few fears still creep into my life, but I don't give them any control because I know I have the power to change them from emotions of insecurity to emotions of love. Anytime you feel that fear has taken up residence in your mind, I encourage you to journal all of your emotions and feel the experience of liberation as you let your fears leave your mind and body. You have the power to heal yourself. Set up the intention with determination. Once you do this, the healing occurs right before your eyes. You are the only one who can make the decision to heal your heart. Nobody can do it for you. Most of the time you may make this decision when the pain is too unbearable. However, you do not have to go to extreme pain. Instead, you just have to learn how to face your fears as they come and quickly release them into the nothingness where they came from. This is self-love. Once you learn to love yourself, you can conquer fears and reap the rewards of all that life has to offer.

Faithful Creation

Many people believe that faith has to accompany religion. There is faith outside religion. Otherwise, would we ever sow seeds if we did not believe with faith that they will grow into flowers, plants, trees or food? Every action you take depends on faith, whether you are willing to admit it or not. Faith is the driving force and principle power behind all creation. Without faith, nothing can exist. You have been given free will to be, do and have what you want. I believe God places desires in our hearts because they are the roadmap to our calling here on earth. To be able to answer that calling you have to have the faith that there is an invisible power working on your behalf. I always say that this power is conspiring in your favor to have the things you want to have, be or do. The secret is to trust in this invisible power the same way a waterfall trusts that water is going to keep flowing from the invisible to the visible world to provide for its existence.

Faith is a power that operates throughout your life and sadly, as you develop your reasoning skills, you tend to disregard faith's importance. As a child you were conditioned to believe only what is visible. As you grew into adulthood, you didn't believe that miracles can happen without the help of the physical world. When you attempt to live by faith and don't see immediate results you backtrack to your original thoughts. Doubt replaces faith and prevents you from realizing your dreams. Fear breeds fear and faith breeds faith.

For a good part of my life, I lived with faith but it was to the outside world and not in God. For years, everything I believed was what I saw with my eyes or my physical world. This was not faith. Because of this lack of faith, my life was a roller coaster and some days were great and other days were terrible. Little by little I came to the understanding that there was a God in control of our lives. The realization that God controlled my life guided me and gave me the power to see that there was a world that I couldn't see with my eyes. My discovery led me to start reading and studying the subject, which opened up my intellect and understanding about real faith. My new understanding taught me that imagination was a part of faith and everything I could imagine I could achieve.

Since your thoughts create your reality, having faith is essential in order for you to accomplish your goals or fulfill your dreams. If you want positive things to happen, then you have to combine faith with imagination. Your imagination is an incredibly powerful tool that paves the way to a new reality. Every day you use your imagination to conceive outcomes. For both good and bad. Sadly, the majority of people only imagine bad outcomes such as "Will my husband and I argue today?" "What will happen if I'm late to work?" Instead of imagining what can go wrong, why not imagine your hopes and dreams coming true? What you imagine tends to happen. You must find ways to shift your focus away from fears and instead focus on faith and what you want to create. The human race has a difficult time believing that miracles can happen every day. You can't try to understand faith or to rationalize it. You can only see the manifestation of faith after you have embraced it. Faith will take you over life's hurdles and guide you to your desired outcome. Faith is the greatest gift you can give to yourself.

A Journey of Faith

Recently, I was privileged to witness my faith manifest on a trip to Ghana, Africa. The board members of our organization, Glorious Being Center and I met one afternoon to discuss our plans for building an orphanage in Ghana based on the self-sustainable system called "permaculture." During that meeting, we set the intention to receive ten plus acres of land in Ghana to carry out our project. Mind you, we didn't have a clue as to how it was going to happen. We consciously worked with the concept of the three steps to manifesting what we wanted in Ghana: 1. Ask. 2. Let go and let God. 3. Receive. When you ask God for something, He doesn't put restrictions on your request. He honored our request according to our faith and expectancy of what we wanted in Ghana. This is why you have to act as if you already have what you have asked for. Each member of the board expected to receive the land donated and this is exactly what happened. After giving Him our intention, our group decided to let go and to allow God to guide us to the appropriate action.

Six months later, we organized our trip to Ghana. On our visit, we met a young man named Gracious Legacy. We took his name as a sign we were supposed to meet him. Our hunch was confirmed when he told us he was an expert in organic farming, which is what our project is all about. Another manifestation of faith was when he told us that he was supposed to have traveled to another city but a little voice told him to cancel his trip. Gracious Legacy canceling his trip was God's way of helping us meet the right people to find our land.

We invited Gracious Legacy to join us in our travels. Along our journey, we talked to him about our plans to have a self-sustainable system with vegetable gardens, fruit trees, livestock, solar energy and all the components of a system where the children were going to have everything they needed right within their land. Creating a self-sustaining residence for the children using the system of Permaculture was very important to us. Through Permaculture, a bond is formed between the land and the people who live on it.

Faith manifested reality again when Gracious met the Director of Permaculture in Ghana on one of our stops. We solicited a scholarship for Gracious Legacy to become a certified Permaculture designer and he granted it to him. Gracious Legacy shared with us that his family owned land in the Volta region of Ghana and promised to take us there. Faith stepped in again because he offered to ask his family if they would donate any of their land to build the self-sustaining residence for the children. He took us to his family and introduced us and we explained to them our reason for being in Ghana. One of the men in his family stood up and told us that he didn't want us to go back to the United States empty handed and instead he wanted for us to get back home with a sense that we had accomplished our original plan. He gifted our organization with 10+ acres of land.

We shook hands and through faith, our trip to Ghana was a success. This miracle would not have happened if we had worried about the final outcome. We were certain that we were going to receive our land. This was unquenchable faith. This is the type of faith you have to have to accomplish anything in life. The Universe wants to support you but you cannot stop the flow by mental doubts or questioning how it is going to happen. The "how" is the domain of God and He is well equipped to give you your heart's desires. He created the entire Universe. You have to believe that there is Divine order at work all the time. Once you ask for what you want, your job is to let go and let God, and open your heart to receive. The guidance will come, and at that moment you must take action. When you are willing to follow Divine guidance, your life turns into a flow of miracles. When you use the muscle of faith, it becomes an avalanche as if the gates are opened.

— Glorious Discovery —

Review of Fears Exercise:

Everyday take the time to do this powerful process to release all your fears. Once you finish, make sure to use this tool to let go of any new fears that may show up.

- Write down who or what you fear. List here situations, people, or principles that you fear.

- Explain the cause. Ask yourself why you are fearful and what is going to happen.

- Express how it affects you. Is it your self-esteem, your security, your ambitions or dreams, your future?

- Let go and forgive yourself for thinking and acting this way.

- Take Responsibility. Make the decision to live your life based on faith by shifting all fear-based beliefs.

- Replace all fearful thoughts, words and actions with empowering ones as soon as they show up in your consciousness. Use affirmations.

- Write down your new reframed story expressing the new you as it if it is already happening and read your new story until you experience the desired results.

Affirm:

- I take responsibility for my life experiences and make changes when necessary

- Loving myself brings harmony to my life

- I forgive myself. I declare myself innocent

- I have the faith that there is an invisible power working on my behalf

- I let go and let God and open my heart to receive

Chapter 8

Embrace Your Essence

Have you ever gotten so entangled in your thoughts and emotions that you lose sight of who you truly are? I spent a good part of my adult life living in direct opposition of my true self.

On May 1st, 2000 I had an experience that totally changed my life. I was celebrating my birthday with friends and we were sharing positive comments about each other. I suddenly felt energy in my body and heart that was filled with a love that was beyond anything I had ever experienced before. I was in total bliss, and I saw a light that was so pure it was almost as if I was looking straight into the face of God. In the room there was a lady who knew about energy and she told me that I was channeling divine healing energy. She asked me if I could do hands on healing for the people who were with us. As I was in this space of ecstasy, I agreed, without knowing what she meant. I put my hand on the forehead of every person and they too felt this divine love that was channeled through my hands. We all felt an unconditional love that is impossible to describe. On my birthday God opened my heart to love His children unconditionally. This is the best gift I have ever received.

After this beautiful experience, I kept feeling this vibration inside of my body and one day I decided to meet with a pastor of a church. After sharing with him my experience, he told me that I received the gift of healing and urged me to put together a healing circle to start sharing this gift with others.

That day, May 1, 2000, when I experienced the true and pure love God has for each one of us, I finally realized my mission in life. As soon as I saw the face of God and He anointed me with the power of healing, my purpose was to teach others that God wants you to love yourself the way He loves you. God doesn't want you to lose sight of His love and His plan for you. He wants you to stop allowing your negative thoughts and past hurts to cloud His divine plan for you. The sooner you understand and accept God's love, the more aligned you become with His Spirit to accomplish any goal or overcome any obstacle.

The majority of people believe that we are just this physical body. The experience that we had that day was a real demonstration of the presence of a supreme being. I used to get very scared when people spoke about things that I did not understand and the term Spirit intimidated me. I automatically thought of ghosts. I did not understand that God is Spirit and if we are made in His image and likeness we must be Spirit too. I cannot exist without the presence of Spirit because it is who gives me life. Every cell in your body is filled with the presence of God. The sooner you understand and accept it, the sooner you can have an intimate relationship with God. I invite you to embrace your true essence and remember that you are Spirit first, and you have a mind and you live in a body.

Your body is the housing or the channel for Spirit to express through you. To develop an intimate relationship with God, all you have to do is know that God is pure love and would never do anything to hurt you. Just think about some of His attributes. For example, love, compassion, patience, humility, kindness, joy, and generosity. As you open your heart to demonstrate these qualities in your life, you develop a beautiful relationship with your Creator. Let go of all negative thoughts and behaviors of fear, worry, envy, and anger. Choose instead to embody God's attributes in your daily life. This is how you embrace the Spirit of God in you.

When I share with people that the Spirit of God lives inside of them, I often sense a feeling of confusion. I understand the feeling because I too once lived oblivious to the fact that God's Spirit resides inside of me. Recognizing Spirit as an absolute truth in your life is vital. You may have just read the previous statement and thought to yourself, *Gloria, why is the realization so important and what does it really mean?* Once you acknowledge and accept the presence of Spirit in you, it becomes a steady force behind all of your thoughts, emotions and deeds.

You are *not* your body or mind. In reality, you are so much more. You are Spirit. You are the pure essence of God. This force flows in and out of you all the time and it is always connected to all there is. I had no idea that I was Spirit and I really regret all of those years living in fear thinking I was my body. By living my life through my body I experienced nothing but limitation and control. I lived in emotional turmoil and tried to control people by telling them what to do and they tried to control me in the same manner. It was a daring game of control. When you live your life thinking that you are just your body, you live in ignorance. Are you the same today as you were at age ten? No, of course not. Your body has matured and grown into adulthood. You look entirely different. You weigh more and if you're like me you probably have a bit of grey hair, too. Along with the physical changes, you've emotionally matured too. Countless thoughts, good and bad, have passed through your mind. Emotions such as fear, anger, happiness, and joy have also been a part of your growth. A few extra pounds and a couple of wrinkles have only changed your appearance. Your body has changed, buy you have stayed the same. Your Spirit is the part of you, which is unchangeable because it's never touched by external experiences.

Your body and mind are subject to the abuses of your thoughts and actions, but your Spirit is not. Your Spirit is immune to past, present, or future hurts. Your thoughts, emotions, actions, and body are of no consequence to your Spirit. As you acknowledge the presence of Spirit within and understand that nothing happens just through your body, you connect to your infinite potential, a world of countess possibilities. Live your life consciously, understanding that you can release all negative emotions lingering from the past and align with your Spirit through reflection and meditation. Before I continue, I want to point out that the recognition of Spirit is only part of the equation. Acknowledging Spirit is like sitting on the sidelines. Not only do you have to accept the Spirit within, but also to know your Spirit. To *know* your Spirit is to embrace your essence regardless of the circumstance you're in or the perspective you view life through.

Through meditation, Spirit taught me that I was made in the image of God and His love for me is unmatched by anything or anyone. By recognizing and getting to know God in me, I was able to release the childhood paradigm that I wasn't good enough and replace it with the truth that I am a perfect child of God. As you develop a deeper understanding of your essence, you can also remind your children and loved ones each day of their divinity and that they are children of God. The more you remind them of their divinity, the more they are going to live in peace and joy and they are going to create a ripple effect with the people around them.

A Magnificent Journey

You are here on a journey and Spirit is the energy that wants to find ways to express itself through you and expand His presence. God wants to experience the world through you. Since you are made in the image and likeness of God and God is love, your essence must be pure love. Your essence is the expression that comes from pure truth, and is an expression of divine love. What is divine love? It is the love of the divine; it is the love of the universe, it is love that is eternal and unchangeable. It is your responsibility to share the love that is within you with every person you encounter. This is how you embrace your essence every day. Unconditional love, humility, patience and generosity are all attributes of your essence. As you operate from the space of love, kindness, generosity and honesty, you become a stronger person and more congruent with your essence. All the struggle, greed, anger, fear and stress begin to dissolve. For a beautiful and peaceful life, you need to have love as a driving force behind your thoughts, words and actions.

What has God given you that you need to take hold of—even if it doesn't look like it from where you're standing? Freedom in finances? A healed relationship? A better marriage? A stable job? A dream He's whispered to your heart? Can you move forward in your essence, counting on the fact that it has been given to you already? "Things are always working out for me" is a wonderful affirmation that you can use to move you in the right direction. Imagine living your life knowing that it's true. When you live with the knowledge that life unfolds as planned, a peace envelopes you.

Every day I set up my intention to be in alignment and totally connected with my essence. God made both you and me from His original form. It is your responsibility to work diligently to align yourself with your essence to find peace and true unconditional love. I believe that every one of us needs to connect with our essence because that is how we will shift into love to impact the collective consciousness of humanity. Every time a human being accepts their essence as a whole it influences the entire human race. This is what all of the great leaders did. They accepted their higher ambition and caused great change in the world. Whatever you wish to accomplish in your life, ask your Higher Power to guide you and show you the way. Remember, you are not your physical body. You are instead only borrowing it. Your body is not your essence; your true essence is pure unconditional love. Align with this essence as you move forward on your magnificent journey.

My journey of awakening to my essence has gifted me with a beautiful relationship with my Creator. I am open and willing to listen to His guidance. Whenever I read a particular book, for instance, I get closer and closer to the source of my being. He places items in your life so you can hear or read the truth about His unconditional love for you. When you are aligned with your essence, the old tapes that replay in your mind about not being good enough or smart enough are erased. Why? Simply because your Spirit is guiding you toward pure love and unconditional acceptance. Anytime you have a destructive thought, tell yourself that you are a child of God and through Him you can do anything.

Embrace Your Power

Too many people spend years, months, days feeling sorry for the things that they didn't do. It is important to always do introspection from the space of love and respect and not from failures of the past or regret or guilt. If I take a look at my life I would see the old Gloria who used to be angry, short tempered, and ignorant. If the old fears showed up, the Gloria of today could handle them from the new perspective and transform them into something good. The secret is to respond to your life's experiences from the space of love, instead of reacting to life. When you are able to respond to life, you open the doors to rewarding outcomes and stepping into your mission on earth. As you embrace the power of your essence, your Creator is able to talk to you, to guide you, and to help you because those fears and anger have faded away and the resistance is gone. Now you are giving way to your connection with Spirit, which is why it is so magical. I know this to be true because I've experienced the power.

When I was not connected to my emotions, I had no clue that my Creator was there or that I could call on Him for guidance anytime I needed to. Now I take the time to meditate and talk to my Creator and ask Him questions. The conversations I have with Him are so fulfilling and magical that

I am always able to get answers to my questions. I learned quickly though that I can't hear any answers if my mind is clouded with anger and doubt. One of the best methods to rid your mind of negative emotions is to face them head on by journaling. Once you've faced them then you can work on releasing them and replacing them with love and forgiveness.

I liken my journaling to looking at the sky. Anytime I see clouds I know that the sun's rays are just waiting to shine and warm the day. Whenever you allow the clouds to restrict conditions, you can't see the sun. However, when you embrace those clouds of emotions and challenges and realize that the sun is there the whole time, then you can experience the light. I can't imagine my life without living God's purpose for me. Once you are able to embrace your essence and be responsible and respond positively to every challenge and obstacle, God's plan for you will be revealed. When I cleared away the clouds and realized my purpose, I was able to ask Him how I was supposed to fulfill my purpose here on earth. As a result of my conversations and my willingness to follow His guidance. I now do what I love the most, to empower people to uncover their glorious being. I do it as a speaker, trainer, coach, healer, minister and humanitarian.

Since my mission has been revealed to me, I continue to study and understand my essence. Each one of you is a being of infinite potential and to develop that potential it is necessary to understand how to unlock it. The more you get to know yourself and better yourself, the more opportunities God gives you to help other people understand who they are. I'm supposed to create a global awakening movement because of the insights my Creator gave me. It is my mission to empower children and people all over the world so they remember and embrace their true essence. As you release any destructive thoughts and embrace the power of your essence, God's mission for you will be revealed. As you let go and let God take control, you will be able to see more clearly God's calling for you and as a result you awake every morning to experience the joy that awaits you.

Once you decide to follow your purpose, it becomes your friend and you will do anything that is in your power to carry it out. To develop your purpose you have to be willing to change the old ways. That's the key. How do you know what you need to change? Well, you take a look at the results in your life. If you are not satisfied with your results, then you make the decision to discover what beliefs or habits you have to change that might be sabotaging what you want. Seek the help of a coach and engage in study programs that will assist you in your journey. It is a day-to-day effort and commitment to stay on your purpose. When you are serious about your mission, Spirit will guide you on how to do it. It is about your decision and discipline to execute the mission that needs to be carried out. It is also persistence and doing what it takes every single day. One of the ways Spirit led me to my mission was by guiding me to start a non-profit organization. I didn't know why. I didn't understand the reason why that was something I needed to do. Fortunately I went to God for a sign and got the confirmation that this was exactly what I needed to do.

As soon as I got the confirmation, people and resources entered my life to create the Glorious Being Center not-for-profit organization in 2004. Any time you have doubts ask for guidance and signs because God will give you the opportunity to see the correct path to take. Some time ago, I asked for a sign about our self-sustaining permaculture system for our project in Ghana, Africa. The message I received was through a quote that I heard in a movie from the patron saint of ecology, St. Francis of Assisi. He said, "Start by doing what is necessary; then do what is possible; and suddenly you are doing the impossible." When I heard this quote, I knew it was a sign from God. Once you receive your messages and listen, paths will open up for you.

There is an infinite power that is conspiring with you to make sure that you have a happy and abundant life. I love the Bible quote, 3 John 1:2, "Beloved, I wish above all things that you may prosper and be in health, even as your soul prospers." That is a powerful message and having God on your side, that's all you need. As you embrace your inner power, you will continue to experience the magic of miracles that will show up in your life. As soon as you decide to have a relationship with that power, your whole life changes. As a matter of fact, God is the CEO of my company. Why is He CEO? It is because I take all questions and challenges to Him to help with the solutions. You can do the same. Surrender everything to God and allow His guidance and wisdom to show you the appropriate action.

— Glorious Discovery —

- Take some time to journal and release any anger or negative emotions to clear your mind. Once your mind is clear, sit in a quiet place and connect with your Creator. Ask Him for guidance in your life. Listen for answers and as you hear them, write them down and follow His instructions.

- Make the decision to take the necessary steps every day, even baby steps, to move in the direction of your mission. If you are not clear about your purpose, these ideas can help you gain some clarity:

  - Think about the things you used to love doing as a child

  - Think about the things you love to do today

  - Ask friends what are the talents they see in you

  - Affirm: "I choose to know my purpose."

  - In meditation ask for guidance

- Remember that you are Spirit first, you have a mind and you live in a body. Your body is the housing or the channel for Spirit to express through you. Allow His love to transform your life and the lives of those around you.

- Embrace your essence moment to moment by affirming, "My true essence is unconditional love."

Affirm:

- I am Spirit. I have a mind. I live in a body
- My true essence is pure divine love
- The presence of Spirit in me is a steady force behind all of my thoughts, emotions and deeds
- I consciously allow my Creator to express His love through me
- Things are always working out for me

Chapter 9

Manifest Your Heart's Desires

Each one of you was born with the birthright to manifest your hearts' desires. However, many people think that it is impossible to have what they want and only a few lucky ones can really do it. If you are filled with negative emotions such as fear, anger or hate, take an honest look at the images going through your mind. Do you have faith that life will get better? Or are stuck in the victim mode? If you experience financial lack, or have health challenges, or relationship issues, I invite you to make the decision to find the help of a mentor, or a personal empowerment program. This is the first step because remember, when you are in the picture, you cannot see the frame.

Professional guidance will help you make the shift. To change what is not working in your life, you have to be willing to examine your limiting beliefs, feel your emotions and release the past in

order to welcome a new life. This process requires effort and commitment. However, the payoff is a life of satisfaction and happiness. I worked on letting go of all my negative emotions that had been making me feel unhappy. I not only transformed my own life but also I have witnessed how the lives of the people around me and my own family have changed. Once I was able to free myself of those negative emotions, I was capable of becoming the person my Creator meant for me to be.

Along with a coach, you can also find a support group where you will hear about people going through similar situations and how they are able to find solutions. Remember that it's your birthright to have, be or do anything you want. If this is not how you are currently experiencing life, all you have to do is become conscious of the limiting beliefs that you have accepted about your life and be willing to make the changes. Observe yourself and pay attention to your feelings, because they are telling you at each moment what you are creating. For example, if you are constantly getting upset, you will create more experiences that will perpetuate this behavior. You have been given the most powerful gift in the universe, your emotions. I call this the GPS, "God's Power System" which lets you know at any moment what you are creating.

I invite you to pay attention to how you feel and shift your thoughts any moment you are feeling sad, angry, disappointed, and judgmental, to thoughts of happiness, love, contentment, praise and gratitude. The highest emotion that you can strive for is love. Make the commitment every day to express this emotion in all your thoughts, words and deeds. You are in control of your life and your emotions. To manifest your heart's desires it is necessary that you commit to living life consciously. This means taking responsibility for every experience in your life and making the changes when necessary.

I use the GPS to let me know where I am at emotionally, and so can you. For example, if you feel sad, you can go for a walk or listen to classical music to shift your mood. If you are angry, write how you feel or close your eyes and talk to God about your feelings and release all your negative emotions. If you feel judgmental, think of an affirmation that you can repeat over and over to take your mind of the critical mode. Do your best to find a way to shift your focus when you are in a negative mood.

Living a conscious life invites you to deal with what is going on inside of you so you don't contaminate your days with anger, sadness, fear and being out of balance. The greatest joy is attained when you make the path of love the highest priority in your life. This is the way you are in tune with your Creator.

The process of living your life consciously means that you have to eliminate all of the negativity surrounding you. Once you take control of your environment, you can now gain back the power to create the life you've dreamed of. For example, I haven't watched the news in many years because I don't want any of the acidity of the media to be in my conscious mind. Instead of the images on television, I entertain my mind with self-empowering books, affirmations and visualizations. The positive images I fill my mind with gift me with a loving and caring attitude. You can change your life through affirmations, visualization, meditation and goal setting.

Say It, Feel It, See It, Believe It

I was willing to be coached because I finally was able to see how badly my life was out of balance. My openness to the suggestions of my coach helped me to turn my life around. One of the most powerful tools that I have incorporated in my daily life is affirmations. I invite you to become friends with them as well. Affirmations have brought me to the place of peace that I am living in now. I was taught about how affirmations could turn my life around, so I decided to practice using them every day. They taught me not to be in a negative attitude and helped me to move into being positive and seeing the glass half full. I am grateful for all of the good things in my life and affirmations combined with gratitude have improved my relationship with my creator. After incorporating affirmations, I let go of the negative language and emotions ruling my life. I quickly learned that I had the power to create whatever kind of life I wanted.

Affirmations have to be in the present tense because the conscious mind doesn't know the difference between the present and the future. By affirming in the future you are delaying your good to come to you. You have to affirm in the present tense with the firm conviction and "make believe" that is happening now. The universe will rush to send you the people, places and things to manifest what you are affirming. Affirmations also have to be positive and they must be said with feeling and emotion. So, for example, if someone is in debt, an affirmation in the present time and positive could be, *I pay my obligations effortlessly and easily. Money comes to me consistently.*

A wonderful affirmation to repeat is, *I love and accept myself exactly the way I am.* Say this affirmation constantly. If you don't believe that you are beautiful, I want you to realize that you are a child of God. God is the pure essence of love, so as a child of God, you should accept yourself exactly as you are. Why? Because God created you in His image. One of the most important affirmations you can tell yourself each day is that you love and accept yourself exactly the way you are. I am loved and respected and I respect others. Another affirmation I use is that God is my faith and the source of my good. I beckon my heart and my mind to the universe. When I am taking a shower I say thank you in advance for all of the blessings coming my way. This fills my heart with the feeling of grace and gratitude. An example of an affirmation you can use when you are faced with health issues is to tell yourself and others that your health is being restored to perfection right here and now. This is a positive affirmation. An affirmation is a message sent to your body through your feelings, which create a vibration and of course with positive vibrations you feel good. It is not possible to feel bad if you are in a space of love. Use affirmations to bring perfect conditions into your life.

I use affirmations for every aspect of my life. I even affirm my gratitude for my house. I know affirmations work miracles. One morning, a car was speeding so fast down my street that the driver lost control, drove his car into my front yard and stopped just short of one foot from my kitchen wall. This was a true miracle brought about by my affirmations because my house was unscathed. I invite you to use affirmations to bring more positive and happy experiences into your life. Infuse your life with positive people, places and circumstances.

Write your affirmations down and place them around the house so that they remind you of what you want to accomplish. For instance, if you have an issue surrounding money, create an affirmation for all the money that is coming to you and affirm that your heart is open to receiving such abundance and wealth. Remember, you can create any affirmation for anything you want in life, whether it is money, health or love. For example, a good affirmation to place around your home is *I am wealthy. I am healthy. I am happy. All is well.* Make sure that you put the affirmation on the mirror in your bathroom and when you look in the mirror repeat the affirmation to yourself. It will be in a place that you can't miss it and that is another way of creating the discipline to hold on to your affirmations.

You can also make a recording of your affirmations and listen to them. For instance, when you exercise, meditate or drive to work, the repetition serves as an autosuggestion to your conscious mind and helps you to stay on track to accomplish your dreams. Repetition clears any limiting paradigms and moves you to a higher level of consciousness. You can also use affirmations as a mantra. For example, you can repeat "I am prosperous" wherever you are and this will keep you on the right path. When I am feeling down or not in a good mood I use the mantra "only love is real" and I keep repeating over and over to help me going in the right way. The other way I use a mantra is to stay focused on the positive when I am surrounded by negativity. I repeat it silently to myself. I keep reminding myself with the mantra of who I am and what I am doing. I also say, "I radiate the love (Joy) of my Divine Presence."

When I go to bed after a day that has been filled with obstacles, I use the mantra that says "All is well" and I keep repeating that phrase over and over. The repetition of this mantra helps me fall asleep with the confidence that the next day will be a wonderful day. The "all is well" mantra also helps when you have a bad dream or can't sleep well. Your mind needs to be nourished with the positive reinforcement that comes from using this mantra.

If you want to lose a bad habit or let go of a negative belief and when you repeat the affirmation you don't believe it, then do it gradually. For example, if you feel that you are not good enough, you can say, "Until recently I used to feel that I was not good enough, now I understand that I was created in God's image and likeness." Or, "I am opening my heart to believe in myself." If you don't know how to do something, open your heart through an affirmation and allow the creator to show you how. You have to be willing to allow an affirmation to grow. If a farmer plants a seed, he has to wait until it grows before he can harvest it. The same is true with affirmations, you have to say them with conviction and believe without doubt that it is going to happen.

Create affirmations each day and place them in obvious spots where you know you'll see them. Set your intentions for each day with the use of affirmations. For example, *I am grateful that my day is full of blessings and miracles.* Affirmations work only if you continuously say and believe them. I have used them in times that are challenging and I have always had success with them. When you work from the inside out and you are not trying to change the other person, you are the one who ends up winning. Affirmations empower you and support you in taking responsibility for your life. This is how you manifest your life's desires, by consciously using language that enriches your life.

Use Your Imagination as a Tool for great Creation

Combining affirmations with visualization is an incredibly powerful method to create your future. For example, let's say that you want more money. Bob Proctor taught me a money affirmation that I love, *I am so happy and grateful now that money comes to me in increasing quantities, through multiple sources, on a continuous basis.* As you repeat this affirmation, exercise your powerful mental muscle of your imagination. Imagine receiving checks or payments in the mail and you depositing them in your bank account. Imagine all the things you are doing with that money and the joy you bring to your life and to others. Visualization plays a big part in anything you do and it aids you in stretching your imagination. It is crucial that we regain our ability to use visualization and imagination to reach our end desires. Our organization is doing it right now. We are building a self-sustainable residence for orphaned children and we are already visualizing the children living in the home. We repeat an affirmation thanking God in advance for their new home, for the gift of being able to live in a clean and safe environment. As you repeat your affirmation, your subconscious mind translates it into a feeling that your body receives as vibration and then your actions will be based on a strong desire to do what you want.

Your mind's use of imagination is a way of affirming and visualizing a set of goals you want to achieve. Your imagination combined with affirmations and visualizations allows you to set the goals and have a firm idea in your mind of what you want. You have to have a clear idea of the goals in your life. Sometimes I don't know what I want and after thinking through my desire, I begin to get an idea of what the goal is and I can then visualize and start affirming it and keep going with it until I have a set goal. If you are not clear about your goals sit down and ask yourself, *what is it that I enjoy doing and what is it that brings great passion to my heart?* What are some of the things that you would like to see changed, to see differently in the world? Asking yourself what you are passionate about helps you create a list of specific goals you want to accomplish.

You have to allow the process to unfold like magic. Once you do your part to affirm, to visualize and to have the right frame of mind, you have to let go and let God. You don't have to be worried about the how, God will take care of that, but you have to set up the goals so that you will know in which direction you will move. If one of your goals is to have a new home (I'm going to make it up right now), then you have to say I'm enjoying my new home. You take time to visualize for a few minutes every day living in your new home. You see the colors, the furniture in each room. You see yourself cooking in your spacious kitchen, resting in the living room and enjoying your beautiful home.

Another action I take is to make my goals unlimited by continuously adding to them in a vision board or vision book. There is no doubt that a picture is worth a thousand words. A vision book is nothing more than a notebook filled with pictures and affirmations you desire in your life. Vision books are a wonderful way to reinforce your visions and the reason is that the conscious mind doesn't know the difference between what is real and what is imagined. You can do one vision book for each area, your family, your business or any other area of your life. Go to the internet and get the pictures for your vision book. Some you have to have permission to use or buy and others you can just copy and use freely.

Pictures really help you to visualize what you want. Give yourself the gift to believe that you can realize every single goal of your life. Put yourself in a position of *aligning with the feeling* of the end desire. How does it feel to have that new home, or the new job or relationship? Does it make you feel happy, satisfied, free? Feel those feelings right now. This is called the law of allowing. You affirm and feel and visualize in advance the feeling of your desire as if it is already here. You believe with all your heart that you have received it. You set up the goals for every segment of your life. Goal setting through visualization and affirmations doesn't happen overnight but little by little you will learn how to set up your goals in a manner that they can be accomplished.

To make sure you live your life at its fullest potential, I encourage you to use daily affirmations and the power of visualization to envision the good you desire. God will be guiding you and showing you the way to your highest calling. As you use affirmations and visualization to bring your heart's desires into fruition, what is wonderful is that you will be aligning yourself with your Creator's will for you. He is the one who placed those desires in your heart.

— Glorious Discovery —

Make a list of the areas of your life you wish to improve and do the following:

- Create a list of goals for each area in your life. Imagine where you would like to be one year, five years, and ten years from now.

- Write an affirmation for each area in the present tense and positive.

- Repeat your affirmations daily.

- Take time to visualize your goals.

- Have unquenchable faith to know that their manifestation is a done deal!

Affirm:

- I use my mind as a tool for great creation

- I pay my obligations effortlessly and easily. Money comes to me consistently

- God is my faith and the source of my good. I am prosperous

- I am wealthy. I am healthy. I am happy. All is well

- Only love is real

Chapter 10

Turn Obstacles Into Opportunities

More than likely, each one of you has experienced some event or circumstance that prevented you from moving forward to accomplish your goals and dreams. No one ever said that life was going to flow smoothly. Without a doubt, you are going to make mistakes and face obstacles no matter how you live or what you do. Early in my life, I learned one important truth: It is not the obstacles I face that matter most, but instead it is how I handle them. Once I made the decision to think of obstacles and mistakes as chances to learn, my life altered dramatically. You see, an obstacle is really nothing more than an observation of where you have to make some changes. In addition to creating awareness, obstacles and mistakes invite you to take responsibility for the results that you are creating in your life so you can let go of what is not working for you. Why is letting go so important?

Simple, because when you hold on all your past mishaps and barriers, you actually create more of the same.

My second divorce taught me to let go of the past. Looking back, I'm very grateful for the opportunity I had to let go of my old behavior and all of the mistakes I made during my marriage. Initially, I was angry and there were many times I was disrespectful not only to others but myself as well. I decided to look into myself and see where that root of anger was coming from and I found out that it was coming from my childhood. I decided to work with my inner child, and with professional help I was able to remove all of the hate and anger from my heart.

After ridding myself of the toxic anger, I changed my focus from anger to forgiveness and the more forgiveness I welcomed into my heart, the more I learned to practice unconditional love. The experience of love and forgiveness helped me move from being a victim to a victor. Once I stepped out of the victim role, I was able to look at my life and see all of my mistakes. Because of my willingness to openly and honestly acknowledge my misgivings, I was able to see how my present had been created by my attitude. It is very important that you become humble and look at your actions and realize that your present is a result of your past decisions.

As you give your very best it becomes easier to come into the space of understanding and acceptance. Doing the conscious effort to remove obstacles, you open your heart to receive divine guidance. With divine wisdom you can definitely overcome any challenge. The ultimate result of releasing the past is that you end up really being there for yourself because your turn your negative experiences into self-acceptance and self-love. The winner is you.

Plan B

What happens when life doesn't work out like you thought it would? What do you do when you planned for life to look a specific way and all of a sudden everything changed? Obstacles and mistakes fell along your path and none of your dreams and aspirations turned out the way you planned. I'm sure you've had moments where you say "I just didn't see it happening." How do you navigate through life in the midst of uncertainty? For me, I find the easiest thing to do is to submit and be obedient and let Plan B come to fruition. My plan was forever altered by the death of my mom. Initially I was distraught and couldn't believe she was taken from me at such a young age. I was in disbelief, I was just a little girl and I needed my mom. When a child loses her mother, she has lost the unconditional love and then she starts asking questions. People lose a lot of time asking questions like I did. "Why me?" That was my conversation that went on for many years. "Why me?" "Why did I get a father that was emotionally unavailable to me?" "Why did I have a stepmother that was so cruel?"

I thought I was entitled to ask questions such as "Why me and how could you do this to me." In actuality, I was hurting myself by asking those questions. Once I stopped questioning my Creator's decision, I looked at her death as an invitation to learn and use the experience to become a better person. My perception of my mother's death may seem a bit difficult for some of you to understand, but I want you to realize that God is faithful and good and He knows what is best for you. You can't live according to your agenda; you have to develop relentless trust.

Trust in the creator with all your heart and don't lean on your own ways. In the midst of a Plan B, you have to have relentless trust that His idea of your life is better than your Plan A. Trust is difficult for so many people because they love to control every aspect of their lives. I know for me I couldn't trust for a very long time. It wasn't until I relinquished control that I could fully trust. When Plan B enters your life, you probably fight it with every ounce of strength you have. You want to hold on to the idea of Plan A. To many, Plan B represents a complete lack of control, which makes them very uncomfortable. Control is an absolute illusion. Not you, me or anyone else is in control.

The Creator is in control. For example, when I went to bed last night, I didn't tell my heart to beat or my lungs to breath. When you're unexpectedly hit with Plan B, drop control and hand over the reins to the Creator. Control entangles you in worry, fear and anxiety. Let go, relinquish control and trust that Plan B might just be the path you're supposed to take. Each step on the path to Plan B is a step of trust and obedience because God is in control. Along with giving up control, you also need unwavering faith. How do you have unwavering faith? By making a constant effort to have communication with God. The closer you get to God and the more time you spend in meditation, the more your faith builds. The uncertainty becomes a bit more certain as your faith grows.

On Eagle's Wings

Overcoming obstacles takes faith and trust coupled with determination and effort. I worked with coaches and read voraciously. As I delved into my assignments and books, I started to believe in God. As a result of my work, I live each day treating others with kindness and respectfulness. I walk the talk because I believe it is my responsibility to be an example of authenticity as I coach others. I released the envy, anger, jealousy and fear, and now I am happy and at peace with my life and my God. When you correct your mistakes your Creator will help you with everything and as you uncover your glorious being you find the magic in you.

Often times, the phrase, "soar like an eagle" is used to motivate and inspire people. The eagle is used for good reason, not only because of their stratospheric flying; they are also fast, possess a keen eye and are extremely coordinated. Eagles are also adept at turning obstacles into opportunities. How, you may be wondering? An eagle knows when a storm is approaching long before it breaks and will fly to a high spot and wait for the winds to come. When the storm hits, the eagle positions its wings in such a manner that the wind lifts it above the storm. While the storm rages below, the eagle soars above the wind and rain. I believe the eagle teaches a valuable life lesson. When you're faced with a storm, rather than trying to escape it, allow the wind to lift you to a new high just as the eagle does. When a storm rushes into your life—and it will at one time or another—rise above it by setting your mind and belief that the storm doesn't have to overcome you. Allow your Creator's power to lift you above any obstacle.

In many cases, there are factors that make some people not want to overcome the obstacles to heal their relationships.

When you face trials and hardship and ask "Why me?" realize that you can't equate the Creator's affection with your affliction. Even before you were born, God had already recognized all the good in you. Every single one of us comes to a point where we encounter an obstacle. You overcome them through a strong belief, relentless trust and unwavering faith. Whenever you face adversity, realize that you are more than just a conqueror. You are a mega conqueror. This world is going to throw everything it can at you, but don't fear because you know that your Creator will take care of you. Like the eagle, you too can overcome any storm and no mistake or obstacle can separate you from the Creator's unconditional love.

Make the Most of Your Learning Experiences

One of the great little known facts about mistakes is that with the right perspective they can actually be really good learning experiences. They are a pre-requisite for any kind of long-term success. I'm a great example of a mistake success story. When I first came to this country I didn't know anything about the language or the culture.

One time I went to the store and bought what I thought was tuna. I made sandwiches and I absolutely loved them. I enjoyed them so much so that the next day I went to the store to buy some more "tuna". Since I couldn't speak English, I looked up and down every aisle for the can. When I found the can I noticed that it had a cat and whiskers on the picture. I thought to myself, *Gloria, you ate cat food!* I could have said this was a mistake and that I shouldn't have come to this country. Instead I told myself that I was going to have the best experience of my life and learn the language of the country and become a good fit into the society that I had chosen. I haven't eaten a cat food sandwich since!

In my work with clients, I've noticed two recurring ideas that keep people in the mistake mindset – fear and worry. I encourage people to not fear making a mistake because it will help them learn what to do to improve their life. Fear is an easy behavior. Change, however, requires a respectable amount of discomfort. Faith takes work on your part. In the midst of your Plan B, are you so fearful that you can't function? Some people operate in a state of fear. I've lived this way and believe me, it is not fun. I've heard so many people talk about their fear problem. They don't have a fear problem; instead they have a faith problem. They lack faith in themselves and their Creator. Human nature makes it easy to fear. Your fears establish the limits of your life. If you fear failure you're never going to take a risk. Don't get stuck and be paralyzed by fear. Whenever you make a mistake, acknowledge the wrongdoing, give it over to the Creator and ask for guidance to turn what you failed at yesterday into tomorrow's miracle.

Worry steals your success mindset as well and paralyzes you when you make a mistake. You can't see straight because worry is pulling you apart. Worry will steal the faith God gave you. Earl Nightingale compares (not factual but his opinion) worry to a dense fog that keeps you from seeing things as they really are. He uses the analogy of a fog that is 7 city blocks wide and 100 feet deep. If this fog were condensed it would fit in a small glass of water. That fog doesn't seem like such a big deal now, does it? I believe that forty percent of what you worry about are things that never happen. Another thirty percent of your worry concerns events of the past that can't be changed.

Another twelve percent of what you obsess over involves your physical health while ten percent of worry is about miscellaneous items. So with those numbers in mind, ninety two percent of your worries are pure fog with no substance at all. You may be thinking, *Gloria, what about the other eight percent?* The answer is simple. We each have our own specific fears that pertain to only us, but it doesn't matter what those fear are. Let go of your worry and let the Creator come in and take the worry out of your life. It may happen for just five minutes and that's okay. Before you know it those few minutes will turn into hours and then to months and then to years. When you create a mindset that it is okay to make mistakes, you will live in the space of compassion instead of beating yourself up with fear and worry.

When you focus on the improvements and lessons learned from a mistake, you reinforce the ability to make mistakes as part of the process and something that is accepted as long as it improves your situation or circumstance. There is no value in worrying about the mistake or dwelling on it after it is done. Failure is an opportunity to learn and grow. Instead of getting angry, frustrated, sad, worried or depressed, none of which will serve any useful purpose, remember that all failures lead to success and the only way a failure is negative is if you ignore the lesson. The next time you perceive that you've failed in something, instead of saying, "Why did I fail?", a more empowering response would be, "What can I learn from this?" or "What strategy can I use next time?" If you want to set goals, take action to achieve them and bounce back from adversity, you must constantly reinforce the concept that "there is no failure, only learning experiences."

Failure Equals Success

One of the main reasons that may prevent you from reaching your goals and desires is your inability to accept failure. Society's perception is that "failure is not an option", which is why so many people don't want to take risks. If you're like most people, you want an insurance plan that any chance you take is going to be a success before you make a commitment. Life doesn't work this way; the reality is that everything you do involves risks. If you don't risk you don't live. You can't become a victim of failure and let it keep you from achieving your dreams. It is unfortunate that so many people give so much credit to success and neglect failure. Failure is an essential ingredient for success.

What is failure to you? Before you answer that question, take a moment and remove any preconditioned thoughts you have about failure. Notice I asked what failure is to you. The definition is different for everyone. The great news about failure is that you can decide what it means to you. For me it means learning and opportunities. There was a time in my life when I defined almost everything I did as failure, in one way or another. Nothing I did was good enough, even my successes were failures. There was also a time in my life when I allowed everyone around me to influence my opinions and actions based on their world view.

When I took control of my thoughts, I stopped that pattern of self-destructive thinking and now it's your turn to do the same.

Instead of perceiving failure as life ending, consider it as feedback. When a toddler takes their first steps and falls, parents don't tell them to stop and discourage them from trying again. No, instead they encourage their child to get up and try again. If only you could do this with the rest of your life. A small child doesn't fail to walk when they fall; instead they learn to walk when they fall. Yet when you fall down, you call yourself a failure. Failure is not the end; it is a temporary and inevitable part of our overall success. It is an important part of the process, not the end of the process.

Failure brought me closer to success. I didn't see failure as the end and quit. Instead I saw failure as an opportunity and let the failure inspire me to do better, find another way, and move forward. I believe in myself and in what I am doing, and let failure hone and sharpen my character, making me a stronger and better person. Failure is a stepping-stone toward your ultimate goal. I stepped out of my comfort zone so many times because it inspired and compelled me to keep moving forward.

Invaluable Lessons and Future Opportunities

When you make a mistake you learn from it and then replace it with a new approach. Some people believe that when you make a mistake that you are a bad person and have to be punished. How many of history's leaders made mistakes? Too many to count. I believe that the word mistake should be removed from the dictionary and renamed learning experience. When you do make a mistake, look at it to see what you can learn and then do something that will be better than what you did. Say that someone found out that I lied to them. Once this comes out I have to decide to become totally honest in everything that I say. What a wonderful experience! At the beginning of one of my relationships, I said something I shouldn't have said and then immediately apologized and promised that I would never use that language again. My actions prevented me from losing an important person in my life.

No matter how big the mistake was, just release it and move on. Make the changes needed to avoid it next time. Put your focus on what you can do for next time, not what you should have done. All these actions will move you forward and enable you to quickly adapt and deal with similar situations in the future and hopefully you will never make the same mistake again.

Don't dwell on mistakes; instead, look beyond them for future opportunities and move forward. What sets successful people apart from unsuccessful people is their decision to turn obstacles into opportunities. One person could grow up in an abusive situation and decide that means they could never be anyone of importance. On the other hand, another person in that same circumstance or worse decides to use the lessons they learned from their experiences to help others, like I did. The first sees their circumstance as a stumbling block that creates impossibility. I used my "obstacle" as a way to relate to people and help them. Same circumstance...completely different outcome.

Becoming conscious of the decisions you make on a day-to-day basis while consciously and carefully choosing to respond to circumstances gives you power. Even if you only pay attention to the decisions you choose on a daily basis, this aspect of personality alone can make all the difference in causing you to be unstoppable. This alone places you firmly on that pedestal with the elite achievers. Circumstance no longer has the opportunity to be an excuse. You have successfully removed "obstacles" from your life.

Rather than hide from mistakes, why not celebrate them? The best life lessons come when you are challenged and pushed to the edge. You really just have two choices when you encounter obstacles and mistakes: you can either let them have their way with you or you can turn them into opportunities to move forward. How do you react to your mistakes and obstacles? It is your response to these difficulties that determines your success. So, whenever you make a mistake, face adversity, or hit an obstacle, remember that it is all right to fail as long as you have a strong belief, relentless trust, and unwavering faith that you can learn a valuable lesson and soar with the eagles. Adversity reveals your true character and is often a forerunner to greater achievement. Are you ready to turn your obstacles into opportunities?

— *Glorious Discovery* —

Whenever you have a new learning experience, please remember the following points:

- Turn every obstacle into a winning opportunity by using your faculty of perception to see the positive in every situation.

- Let go of what you perceive as mistakes. Let go of the past and forgive yourself. Focus on the good to attract more good into your life.

- God has the perfect plan for you. Release the control and allow divine guidance to lead your way.

- Soar like an eagle. You are bigger than any storm. You have the power within you to conquer your dreams. You are a mega conqueror.

- Make the most of your learning experiences. Be grateful for what you have learned from the challenge and use the feedback as a basis for maximizing opportunities.

- Step out of your comfort zone and move forward in faith to meet success.

- Be unstoppable. Become conscious of the decisions you make on a day-to-day basis and use the faculty of reasoning to turn obstacles into opportunities.

- Anytime you encounter an obstacle or feel like a failure, use affirmations.

Affirm:

- I'm moving from the space of the obstacle to a space of unconditional love and guidance

- Creator, open my eyes to see

- Open my ears to hear

- Open my mind to understand

- And open my heart so I may receive compassion

Chapter 11

Allow the Magic in You to Come Alive!

It is easy to think that 'magic' just happens to some and not to others, but that is not the case. You create the reality you are currently experiencing and that means you can create a magical life! I am not just telling you this to make it sound easy; far from it, I am telling you this because I know it to be a fact that I have experienced in my own life. The way the magic came alive for me was through the daily application of the principles and exercises contained in this book. So don't think that it can't happen to you, it can, but you can't sit around hoping for things to change. You must take control over your thoughts and then take action!

I'll be the first to say it's anything but easy. In fact, for me to be able to experience the transformation in my own life, it has taken discipline, determination, perseverance and a great deal of faith. It didn't 'just happen' and there were times that I honestly didn't see any way for things to work out – but they did, and the rewards far exceeded my effort and commitment.

Your magic will come alive for you as well, but it starts with the realization that any and all change starts with you. Gandhi once said that you have to be the change you want to see in the world, and that still holds true. Each one of us has to come to the understanding that only by working on our own issues and healing them one by one, can we then help others. Each one of us has to take responsibility to clear the walls of resistance to unconditional love. For some of us it is fear, doubt or judgment. For others it could be lack of forgiveness or even hatred due to past events or old hurts. Some might experience it as a lack of self-esteem, insecurity, or lack of self-love. As we each heal, at our own pace and along our individual journeys, we embrace our divine essence - the magic in us.

As you become conscious of the habits or limiting beliefs that you have to change within yourself, and you take responsibility for doing your part every day, the magic in you comes alive. You uncover your glorious being and your true essence within your heart emerges, which is "Agape Love" (unconditional love).

Once this transformation occurs, something truly magical happens: you become a beacon of transformation for others. This is exactly what happened in my family. I was brave enough to put the effort into making the changes from within myself, and my family witnessed this change through my new behavior. Many of them saw how my life had drastically changed for the positive and decided to join me by taking the steps to shift their own limiting ideas and beliefs that were holding them back.

Your individual transformation creates a ripple effect of unlimited magnitude through all those you know or encounter each and every day. History is replete with stories of how brave regular individuals like you and me made an indelible mark in the lives of the people who knew them and then across the broader spectrum of humanity. This may sound like quite a lofty or unattainable idea, but all you need to remember is that it very simply starts with you. Begin with one idea to make your life better and then take that next step the following day to make life even better, and so forth. In this way, the magic expands into your family, community, city, country, continent and eventually, the world as a whole. This is the power of the ONE.

Each one of the chapters in this book contains the answers to releasing and embracing your glorious being. But it must be applied every day in order to keep moving forward. A systematic and focused commitment can provide extraordinary results.

For now, just make this commitment: Each week set the intention to study one chapter of this book starting with chapter one. Keep a notebook as you do this and write down the "Glorious Discoveries" that speak to you from that chapter. Commit to practicing the concepts and exercises daily during that week. Read that same chapter every day for seven days to solidify the ideas within your subconscious mind and keep a journal of your feelings and experiences with each one of the exercises. Do the same the next week with the next chapter until you complete the entire book over a period of eleven weeks.

One tip to put the ideas into practice is to record the "Glorious Discoveries" for each chapter on your phone or iPod and as you listen to the instructions, choose one or a couple of the concepts to practice that day. You can also write them on 3x5 cards and take one card with you every day and commit to practicing the idea with feeling and faith.

Affirm your greatness through the power of your thoughts, your spoken word and your actions. It is in the application of the ideas contained in this book that will help you understand and then experience the realization of your greatness.

The best way for you to allow the magic within you to come alive is to embrace the knowledge that you are going to do an amazing job, and that you will have a victorious transformation. Set up your mind to win and you will!

Repetition is the first law of learning. It is crucial to understand that as you study and practice these concepts every day, the power of repetition will automatically shift your limiting paradigms. What is required of you is your commitment, discipline and determination. Be patient and loving during the process, knowing that the seeds you are planting now will grow and you will reap a very rich harvest.

One point to note is that as you are going through this process of uncovering your glorious being, it is necessary to be very humble because that's how you will open your heart to heal. There are things in every person's past that were painful and there are times when we each inflict pain on others either intentionally or otherwise and you have to work through these emotional road blocks.

You can't skip them or take shortcuts because you will never get past it unless it's dealt with once and for all. It is scary to open those wounds sometimes, but if you really want change you must be brave and humbly accept past events and actions for what they really are.

When you are open, you are willing, which is all it takes to create change. Your willingness to uncover all the good as well as the bad will give you the opportunity to forgive and let go of the past. It will happen gradually, allowing you to celebrate your victories as you experience them. Accepting your greatness takes a lot of humility. God is not confused about who you are and you aren't fooling yourself by trying to hide things. He wants you to align your thoughts with His thoughts of love, peace, and greatness. As you accept His invitation, you become obedient and humble. It is a gift you give to yourself.

I encourage you to use the healing power of journaling as a tool to honor your emotions. At times you are going to be disappointed, angry, fearful, lonely, doubtful or even depressed, and this is when the great practice of writing your emotions will provide an avenue to release those feelings. It is a very safe and healthy way to let go of anger, sadness, and any emotion that might be blocking your joy. You can also write about your victories and positive experiences; then it acts as a reminder of the high points when you otherwise might feel a little low.

Make it a daily practice to write for ten to fifteen minutes about your feelings. Don't judge your negative emotions, just embrace them and see them as a warning sign that is helping you to let go of any resistance to your good. Commit to listening to these emotions by expressing them on paper so you may understand what they are telling you. You can also journal about your family, relationships, work, and connection with your Creator or anything else in your life that you feel is important. At the end of your writing for each day, I want you to pause for a moment. Close your eyes and take a deep breath. Now say, "I release these feelings and thoughts to the light. I embrace my true essence, which is love." Then let go of those emotions and feelings you just wrote about. Leave them on the page; don't keep carrying them around like unnecessary baggage!

Affirmations Are Critical

Another wonderful practice that can support you on your journey of allowing the magic in your life to emerge is the use of affirmations. I can't stress how important and helpful affirmations are to changing your habitual thought patterns. You must repeat them every day with the intention of sending positive autosuggestions into your mind.

This daily dose of positivity is like a vitamin for your brain and keeps old negative thoughts at bay while you are working toward your new attitude and new life.

Remember that affirmations are positive sentences written in the present tense – they are not stated as a wish or dream, but instead are statements of fact about the things you expect to be. They continually send a positive message to your subconscious mind each time you repeat them, and by doing so with feeling and faith, they create outer transformation in your life. The best way I have found to create affirmations is to turn any challenges or negative phrases that you may normally think or use into a positive declaration. For example, if once in a while you find yourself speaking negatively, such as in the sentence, "I don't have enough _____ to _____ (fill in the blanks)", you replace it with an affirmation, "I always have enough _____ to _____ (fill in the blanks)". So if you catch yourself saying (or thinking) something like: "I don't have enough money to go on vacations." Instead say, "I always have enough money to go on glorious and memorable vacations."

It takes a little practice to develop the specific affirmations that speak to you, but I encourage you to do so because the more emotional connection you have to the affirmation, the more positive effect it will have on your life. To get you started, I've included this list of examples but only use these at first. Work each day on new affirmations that have specific meaning to you.

- I affirm in the present what I choose for my future

- I am always there for myself

- I am awesome. I am important. I make a difference.

- I am a gift to the world.

- I am grateful for all the blessings in my life

- I am now creating only self-empowering thoughts, habits and experiences

- I am now open and receptive to my highest good

- I am now using, on a daily basis, tools that support me in embracing my greatness

- I am Spirit. I have a mind. I live in a body

- I believe in myself

- I create my paradise here on earth

- I embrace my greatness

- I forgive myself. I declare myself innocent.

- I give myself permission to dream, to play and to have fun

- I honor my emotions, They are my doorway to freedom

- I live in an ocean of abundance

- I live in the present and consciously create an abundant life moment to moment

- I love and accept myself exactly the way I am

- I take responsibility for my emotions

- I treat people with kindness, love and respect

- I use my mind, words and actions as tools for great creation

- My new behaviors express the love, respect and compassion I have for myself and others

- My thoughts, words and actions are in harmony with who I am

- I radiate the love (joy, abundance, peace) of my Divine Presence

- Only love is real

I shared in the previous chapters how I grew up influenced by the fear and limiting beliefs of my parents and because I was only a child, I did not know any better, so I accepted what they gave me. This happens to all of us to some extent because as children we haven't learned to filter what we are told by adults or other authority figures in our lives. They may be parents, family members, teachers, clergy or others.

Only years later, after the pain of repeating their same patterns, I realized that I had the power and free will to make some changes from within myself. I also knew it was up to me to make those changes if I really wanted to have different results in my life. No one could do it for me. This is when I understood that it was time to make new life-giving agreements with myself and to let go of the self-destructive habits and ideas that I had adopted for years. For example, I criticized myself and others frequently. I took things personally and became angry a lot. I reacted to people instantly and did not think of the consequences of hurting them when I said unkind things. I felt fearful and insecure in many situations in my life. In short, I was out of alignment with my true essence. It is impossible to have a balanced life if you are not aligned with the attributes of God, including love, peace, joy, faith, humbleness, generosity and joy.

It is crucial that you make the commitment to yourself to change your perception of who you are, if this perception is negative. You are not the fear, doubt, debt, anger or anything else that may be in your life right now. You are a pure child of God and your essence is Divine. The best way to change a negative perception is to demonstrate the attributes of God in your daily living. This is the only path to embrace your greatness. You have to take responsibility for the thoughts you think, the words you speak and the feelings that you harbor in your heart and in doing so, you acknowledge that you can change. Your thoughts and feelings must be in alignment with the essence of love, integrity and joy. You must commit to have an impeccable heart. This is the road to true greatness.

A powerful way to support yourself in this journey is to use conscious language, which is language that edifies, praises and affirms your magnificence. To use conscious language all you have to do is observe yourself through personal awareness and any time you are about to say something negative, pause and then replace it with something positive. No one forces comments out of your mouth, which means you must create the self control to think before you speak because once something negative is said it cannot be taken back.

Here are some ideas on how to practice conscious language: Use phrases that start with *I Can, I Am, I Will, I Choose, I Have, I Love, I Create, I Enjoy, I Imagine.* Commit to using this empowering language in all your conversations.

It is also essential to reemphasize the importance of surrendering to a higher power on a daily basis. You need to lean on that power and trust that it will guide you in the right direction. By harnessing that higher power, it will support your efforts and help you to truly attain inner peace. The reason this occurs is because as you let go of the need to control, God can guide you and reveal His plan for you and you will be able to fulfill His highest calling.

Many people find it hard to surrender control of their daily lives, but it becomes easier with practice. To surrender to Spirit here are some steps you can take:

- Meditate every day for at least 15 minutes

- Walk in nature

- Listen to classical music or soft music

- Read, listen and watch uplifting messages

- Demonstrate the attributes of the Creator, which include love, peace, generosity, joy and kindness in everything you think, speak and do.

- Journal by expressing your emotions in writing

Meditation for Real People

Now, I realize not everyone understands or knows how to meditate. The whole idea is to simply quiet the mind for a few moments and allow peace to settle over your heart. I'm sure you have experienced times when it seems your mind is running a thousand miles per second. You have probably even been kept up at night at times because your mind is running on overdrive! I know I have! It is telling you it needs rest and you can acquire this rest through meditation. You don't need to be in a certain place or a certain time, although having a regular quiet place and time for meditation does help. But it can also be done anywhere, anytime you need a moment of peace. It can be in the car while waiting on children, or in the doctor's office waiting on an appointment, or even in the washroom! Anywhere you can stop, relax and quiet your mind for a minute or even up to 15 or 30 minutes – take the moment of peace where you can get it! But also plan longer times to meditate to experience the deeper peace it will bring you. I know in my own life, meditation has brought me understanding and has given me profound peace. It has been said that in meditation you are able to silence your mind to catch the thoughts of God. What a wonderful reward for quieting your mind and letting go.

Here are some tips to enjoy your planned meditation times:

- If you feel that it will help you to relax your mind, light up a candle or play very soft music. Know that you cannot do it wrong because meditation is your personal connection with your Creator. Make the commitment to remain in silence for at least 15 minutes. You can set up a timer if you want but the idea is to empty your mind, not watch the clock.

- Start by closing your eyes and be willing to quite your mind to the best of your ability.

- Imagine that you are in a "secret place" (A garden, the beach, the mountains, the forest) where you have an appointment with your Higher Power.

- Take a few deep breaths inhaling the feeling of unconditional love and well-being. Exhale and release all concerns, fears, and judgment. Be willing to surrender all challenges to your Higher-Power.

- During this period you can imagine that you are in the company of beings of light, angels and God. You can imagine God as light, or an Angel, or a Divine Presence. Ask this Presence any questions you may have and wait in silence for the answer. You might receive just a word or a couple of words as an answer.

- You can read a quote from a sacred book before you start your meditation and then set up the intention that you are going to receive revelation or inspiration or a deeper understanding of the quote.

- Before you leave your meditation, thank God for His blessings and then open your eyes and right away journal anything you received or any emotions that came up for you.

- Affirm: "Because I choose to take the time to meditate every day, I enjoy a deeper connection with God."

When I talk to people about meditation and bringing peace into their lives, invariably someone will say, "But that is not possible in my life, it's absolute chaos! There is no way!" or they may say, "That just won't work, I can't empty my mind and even if I did, it doesn't change anything." But that isn't true. Peace and mental quiet are essential for dealing with the chaos of everyday life. I know you have experienced life that runs at a frantic pace – we all have. The problem is that if your mind and heart are also frantic, it just feeds the chaos. Before you know it, life is spinning out of control. Meditation isn't pretending life doesn't exist or that there aren't very difficult things to deal with sometimes. It is a tool that allows you to exist in the midst of complete chaos and not be destroyed by it. It gives mental strength and stability and allows you to see solutions and ideas that you otherwise wouldn't.

Live in the Present

Another very important tool to dealing with stress and chaos is to live in the present. So often, we are stressing over the past, or worrying about the future. So much so, that we forget to enjoy the present. Have you ever felt that first blast of cool autumn air and wondered, "Where did summer go?" It feels like you missed it, and you did because you weren't fully present to enjoy all that summer had to offer.

I will often hear parents lament, "Just yesterday my child was a baby, but now they are going off to college and I feel like there were so many things I didn't fully enjoy while they were little." This happens to us all on one level or another. We get so wrapped up in getting things done that we miss out on what is really important and valuable. The cure for this is to live fully present each and every day.

To live in the present means to enjoy each moment and be willing to let go of the temptation to dwell over the events that happened in the past or worry about the future. It means focusing your attention only in this moment. I invite you to make the commitment to savor each moment as if you are enjoying the most delicious meal in the world. Don't worry about the small things! If you are wondering what constitutes 'small things' ask yourself, "Will this matter five years from now? When I am at death's door will I regret doing (or not doing) this?" This will show you that virtually everything that is not supporting or enjoying the ones you love, or living the purpose the Creator intended for you, is 'small stuff'. The dishes can wait, the yard can grow another few inches, and that email from work won't change the world. Let it go.

Living in the present gives you the opportunity to put the energy necessary to finish each project with joy and ease. You aren't overwhelmed worrying about what happened yesterday or what needs to get done tomorrow, you are fully focused on right now. With each task or event you are fully present, fully focused and reaping the full rewards. By living our whole lives in this manner, we are more aware of the constant and available guidance that gives us small nudges each day toward our greater purpose.

I know we all like to think that the stress in our lives is external, but that's not true. Sometimes we put pressure on ourselves and rush through life, not realizing that there is no reason to hurry. It is much like when many people are all trying to get on an airplane. Some may rush and hurry and become agitated. Others may stroll along and enjoy every moment, but they will all arrive at their destination at the same time. Such is life. We each have 24 hours in the day. Some rush through it stressed, angry and worried; others enjoy all each day has to offer and live in peace by existing in that moment. They each still have the same 24 hours.

I invite you to be fully present each day and not worry how long your journey to change might be. It's not a race and each of us arrives exactly when we are supposed to. Simply embrace one step and go from there. One way to remind yourself to take one step at a time is to remember that in the spiritual world there is no time. There is only this moment. So as you approach each task each day while fully focusing on doing your best, you open yourself to the flow of miracles and guidance.

It takes discipline to keep your mind from going many different directions, but with practice you will be able to exert more self control over your mind than you ever thought possible. As you live each day taking one moment at a time, you are able to stay peaceful and connected to the stream of good that is all around you.

Choose Gratitude and Love

It is interesting what effect the simple act of gratitude can have on a person's outlook. The truth is that it is impossible to harbor negative feelings while experiencing gratitude for all that life offers. Gratitude is a state of being that connects and aligns you with the feeling of love and joy and as such, repels anything negative. You can think of it as 'Life Armor'. When you are experiencing trouble or difficulties, that is the time to think of all the things in your life that are good and true. This will allow you to step back from the situation at hand and feel the emotions of love and joy. But gratitude is not just for when times are hard.

Being grateful each day, and planning a time each day to think on things you are grateful for, keeps your heart open and receptive to your highest good. As you open your heart to give, you open yourself to receive. I'm sure you have experienced giving at some point and for most people, it usually happens that they get more out of giving to someone else than they do out of receiving. That is how gratitude works. It opens this porthole to let more good into your life and you will receive abundantly.

Even as we have challenges, these make us stronger and give us the character and discipline to persevere. The more grateful you are for absolutely everything in your life, including all your challenges, the more blessings you receive. It is for this reason that you want to keep your feelings of gratitude circulating; like a waterfall gives its water fully and unconditionally, living with an attitude of constant gratitude opens the gates of heaven and your blessings will flow like a torrential river.

As you can guess by having read this book, we choose everything in our own lives including our emotions. Just like with gratitude, you get back what you give when it comes to love, so it is useless to wait around for someone to show up and love you. You have the choice to love yourself and then give that love to others. As you give, you then receive – not the other way around!

Choosing love is a decision that we must make moment to moment and it isn't always easy. But the price that we pay when we choose the opposite of love, which is fear, could be very devastating. It can affect our finances, our relationships and our health. Just as one little pebble sends ripples out over the whole surface of the water, one small decision to choose love can do the same. I challenge you to focus on this one idea and choose love every day, every hour for one week straight. Smile at people, help strangers, wait patiently (this is really a hard one!), and focus on how grateful you are to be able to chose the life you are going to be leading. Every day, notice the change in people you spend time around. Do they smile more? Laugh more? Ask if you got a new haircut or new clothes? Comment that there just seems something different about you or that you are noticeably happier? They will notice, which means you attitude up to this point has affected them and not necessarily in the most positive way. As you go through each day, notice how much easier life seems to be. People feel your good will and respond in kind which means by choosing love, you have chosen to make your life easier and more peaceful – and it can happen in as little as a few days!

Truly we are in control of our future and the quality of our lives. The decisions we make today that are based either in love or fear will determine what you will experience tomorrow. The secret is to choose wisely. To choose wisely all you have to do is choose to be happy and peaceful instead of wanting to be right all the time, or the smartest person in the room, or the one in control of everything.

Of course, it's not quite as easy as I'm making it sound, just as letting go of fear can be difficult at first. Choosing love is a way of being which requires practice. The good news is that the more you practice, the more you form the habit. As you form the habit, you start experiencing the good results and this propels you to keep choosing love via positive reinforcement.

Know that by choosing love you are in alignment with the Spirit of God within you, which is everyone's innermost desire as it allows them to be all they were intended to be. This alignment brings peace, joy, love and fulfillment, which is what we are all intimately seeking. The best news, and the idea I most want you to take away from this book, is that it is completely within your control to choose this alignment. I encourage you right now to take that first step toward creating the life you desire – it is fully within your reach.

My prayer for you is that you continue to open your heart to uncover the *Glorious Being* within and find the *Magic in You*. This is self-realization!

About the Author

Gloria Ramirez, MBA, is an amazing speaker and an outstanding seminar leader. Her passion is to inspire individuals to uncover their *Glorious Being* so they find the magic in them. She is also a certified coach, a minister and a healer, known as the "Extraordinary Life Transformer." She guides people to recognize any limiting beliefs preventing them from accomplishing their dreams and shows them how to replace them with empowering habits. Gloria's life is an example of triumphantly overcoming obstacles. Her loving and compassionate personality and her intuitive skills remarkably create tangible results in people's lives.

Gloria is also a humanitarian. In 2004, she founded Glorious Being Center, a non-profit organization devoted to empowering children and women to greatness. She is a Platinum Member of motivational speaker Les Brown's network and is also a Certified LifeSuccess Consultant through Bob Proctor. Because of Gloria's charisma, passion, zest for life and authenticity, her teachings transform people from the inside out. She lectures internationally in the fields of personal development and spirituality. She is the host of the well-acclaimed weekly talk show, "Thank God it's Monday." www.GloriaRamirez.com

www.ingramcontent.com/pod-product-compliance
Lightning Source LLC
Chambersburg PA
CBHW021400090426
42742CB00009B/940